T0285825

The 500 Hidden Secrets of
MILAN

INTRODUCTION

This book invites you to experience the real Milan, including its lesser-known sides. It will help you discover garden districts as well as rationalist architecture, and art nouveau neighbourhoods as well as very recent skyscrapers by starchitects. You'll also be motivated to go and explore the growing areas outside of the centre that have become popular in recent years like Porta Venezia, Isola and NoLo. The gentrification of these neighbourhoods has brought about interesting initiatives and spaces such as art galleries and concept stores. These are hip places-to-be but they also stay true to that understated, low-key vibe that's so typical for Milan.

The aim of the selection is to arouse the reader's curiosity but above all to help visitors experience the city like a local. This book advises you to take a sunbath at a beautiful seaside resort from the 1930s or to look at the view from the window of a design institution. You'll be able to try a new bistro or learn where the 'almost private' cult movie screenings are. This guide also reveals the secrets of a museum house, and tells you about a church that hides contemporary artworks. It will lead you through the streets of historic Milan where you can shop but in the meanwhile also take a peek, through the doors, at unique halls and courtyards. Many of the addresses and facts in these lists bear witness to the great changes that have taken place in recent years (and they give a preview of future ones); however the not-to-miss classics also get the attention they deserve. Of course a selection like this can always cause debate; in the end it's the result of personal choices made by the author. She has made these choices with great care and authenticity.

HOW TO
USE THIS BOOK?

⸺

This guide lists 500 things you need to know about Milan in 100 different categories. Most of these are places to visit, with practical information to help you find your way. Others are bits of information that help you get to know the city and its habitants. The aim of this guide is to inspire, not to cover the city from A to Z.

The places listed in the guide are given an address, including the neighbourhood, and a number. The neighbourhood and number allow you to find the locations on the maps at the beginning of the book: first look for the map of the corresponding neighbourhood, then look for the right number. A word of caution: these maps are not detailed enough to allow you to find specific locations in the city. You can obtain an excellent map from any tourist office or in most hotels. Or the addresses can be located on a smartphone.

Please also bear in mind that cities change all the time. The chef who hits a high note one day may be uninspiring on the day you happen to visit. The hotel ecstatically reviewed in this book might suddenly go downhill under a new manager. Or the bar considered one of the '5 best places for aperitivo' might be empty on the night you visit. This is obviously a highly personal selection. You might not always agree with it. If you want to leave a comment, recommend a bar or reveal your favourite secret place, please visit the website *the500hiddensecrets.com* – you'll also find a lot of free tips and the latest news on the series there – or follow *@500hiddensecrets* on Instagram or Facebook and leave a comment.

THE AUTHOR

Silvia Frau lives in Milan. Her work as a journalist – she writes about travel, food and lifestyle – brings her to every corner of her hometown Milan. She goes everywhere by foot: from newsrooms to conferences, from exciting presentations of new initiatives to vernissages that are often hosted in places that are little known to the public.

Her curious attitude makes her take a new road whenever she has the opportunity; she'll always pop in the new flower shop she discovers on the way, or have a coffee in that beautiful historic bakery that caught her eye. During the winter Silvia loves to work in one of the small local libraries in the city; when the temperatures rise she takes her laptop to a public park or to one of Milan's comfortable co-working spaces with a garden.

Whenever friends come to visit Milan, or friends of friends, they turn to Silvia to ask for tips – most of all she gets asked to share some good food-places. She likes to help them out by writing thematic lists. In this case, however, she is the one who's grateful to those who helped her by giving tips, and to the many friends and colleagues who wanted to share their favourite secret places with her. She thanks photographers Massimo Ripani and Giovanni Simeone for capturing the essence of Milan so well. And last but not least Dettie Luyten, from Luster, for having thought of including the Lombard capital in the series and for having guided her through all the phases of the project with enthusiasm.

MILAN

overview

10
North-West
including **Chinatown**
and **Isola**

3
Centre:
Cairoli *and* **Castello**

8
West

4
Centre:
Sant'Ambrogio

9
South-West
including **Navigli**
and **Porta Genova**

5
North-East
including **NoLo** *and*
Porta Venezia

1
Centre:
Brera, Corso Garibaldi,
Porta Nuova *and* **Porta Venezia**

6
East

2
Centre:
Duomo, San Babila, 5vie,
Ticinese *and* **Porta Romana**

7
South-East

Map 1

CENTRE

BRERA-CORSO GARIBALDI,
PORTA NUOVA *and* PORTA VENEZIA

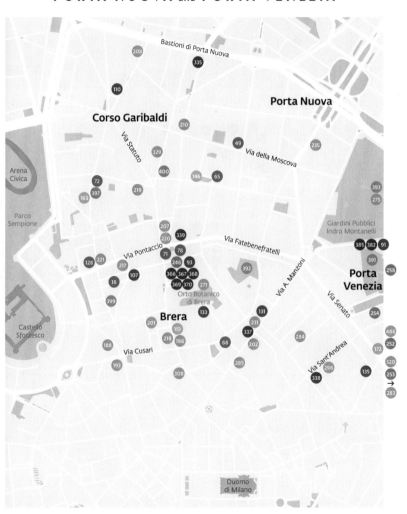

Map 2
CENTRE
DUOMO, SAN BABILA, 5VIE, TICINESE
and PORTA ROMANA

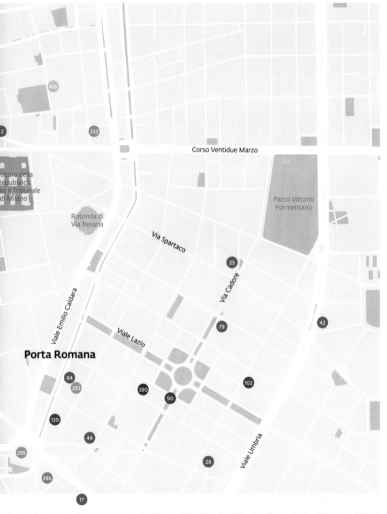

Map 3
CENTRE
CAIROLI-CASTELLO

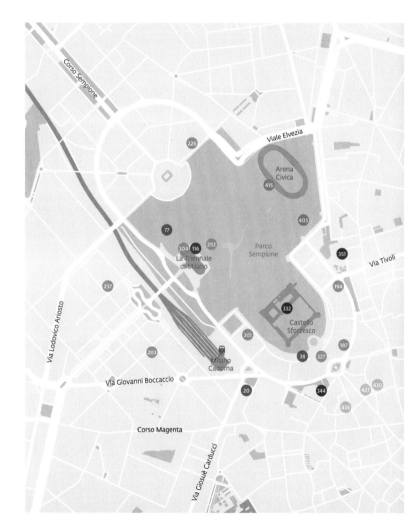

Map 4
CENTRE
SANT'AMBROGIO

Map 5
NORTH-EAST
including **NOLO** *and* **PORTA VENEZIA**

Map 6
EAST

Map 7
SOUTH-EAST
including **TICINESE**

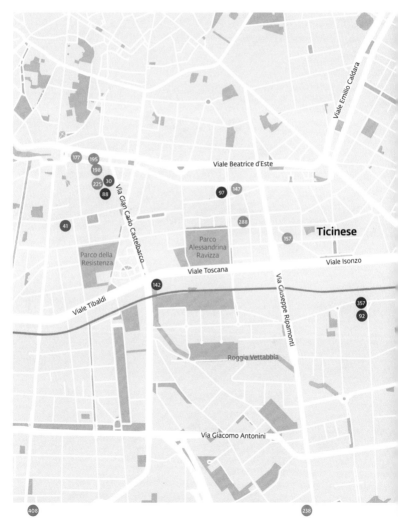

Viale Emilio Caldara

177 195
198
225 30
88

Via Gian Carlo Castelbarco

41

Parco della
Resistenza

Viale Beatrice d'Este

97 147

288

Parco
Alessandrina
Ravizza

Viale Toscana

142

Ticinese

157

Viale Isonzo

Via Giuseppe Ripamonti

357
92

Viale Tibaldi

Roggia Vettabbia

Via Giacomo Antonini

408   238

EAT – **DRINK** – SHOP – FASHION & DESIGN – BUILDINGS – DISCOVER – **CULTURE** – CHILDREN – SLEEP – WEEKEND – RANDOM

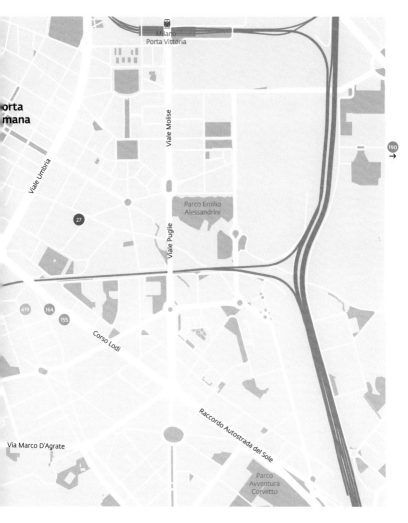

Map 8
WEST

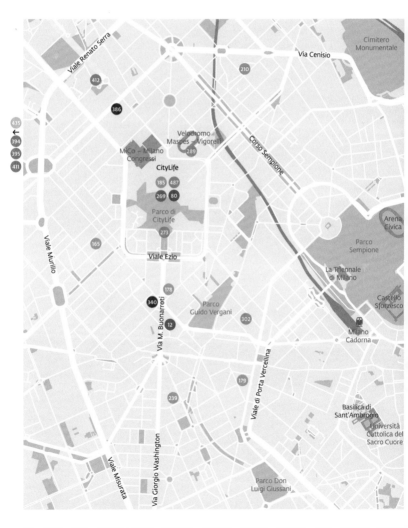

Map 9
SOUTH-WEST
including **NAVIGLI** *and* **PORTA GENOVA**

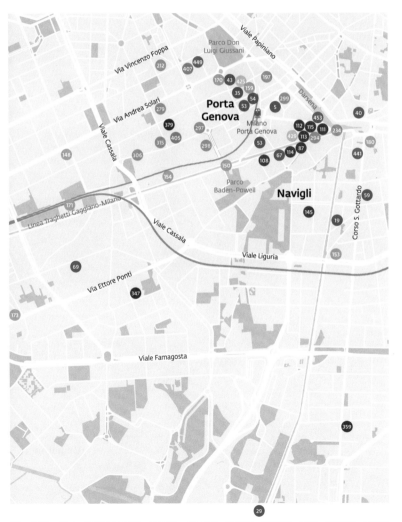

Map 10
NORTH-WEST
including CHINATOWN and ISOLA

Maggiolina

Isola

Cimitero
Monumentale

Milano
Porta Garibaldi

Viale Edoardo Jenner
Viale Marche
Viale Zara
Viale Stelvio
Via Valtellina
Via Alserio
Viale Zara
Via Pola
Via Melchiorre Gioia
Via Ceresio
Viale Francesco Crispi

355 263 60 140 244 168 262 141 123 15 34 350 265 444 86 265 310 21 325 450 265 174 227 199 268 89 445 26 250 451 109 132 316 432 136 160 232 318 184 37 349 305 438 260 196 arco icolò varino

EAT – DRINK – SHOP – FASHION & DESIGN – BUILDINGS – DISCOVER – CULTURE – CHILDREN – SLEEP – WEEKEND – RANDOM

85 PLACES TO EAT OR BUY GOOD FOOD

5
BAKERIES
to check out

---

1 **GRISSINIFICIO EDELWEISS**
Via Teodosio 27
East ⑥
+39 02 7063 0084

What an addictive place this is. Start with one breadstick and before you know it, you'll have eaten half a dozen. They bake breadsticks here daily and every customer has their favourite flavour, including with water, oil, or herbs. And then there are the specials, with salt. Yum!

2 **MERCATO DEL DUOMO**
AT: GALLERIA VITTORIO EMANUELE II
Piazza del Duomo
Duomo-San Babila ②
+39 02 8633 1924
ilmercatodelduomo.it

The huge suspended bronze olive tree, by British artist Adam Lowe symbolises the Mediterranean food and wine culture which you can taste here, from 500 square metres of food counters, with local products and producers that were selected together with the University of Gastronomic Sciences of Pollenzo. Here you can find Grazioli's bread, made with ground organic flour and sourdough.

3 **PANDENUS**
Via Tadino 15
Porta Venezia ⑤
+39 02 2952 8016
pandenus.it

The first branch opened years ago in Via Tadino, followed by three others. A cosy atmosphere, newspapers, freshly cut flowers, and, from morning till evening, baked goods that are produced in house.

4 CONSORZIO VIALEDEIMILLE

Viale dei Mille 1
East ⑥
+39 02 3657 6080
*consorzio
vialedeimille.it*

The bread sold by the Vialedeimille Consortium is produced in the bakery of Milan's Opera men's prison. Buy it here, along with pizza, focaccia and many other natural and artisanal products, from Tuesday till Saturday. They also sell products from the prisons of San Vittore and Bollate here.

5 MICHETTA

Corso C. Colombo 11
Porta Genova ⑨
+39 392 628 7742
michettamilano.it

In Italy there are many types of bread. The bread of Milan is called *michetta*, although nowadays it's difficult to find. It is 'blown', meaning it is empty inside and smells heavenly. Here they pair it with local flavours: Pasini's cured meats, Cascina Selva cheese and San Colombano wine, the only urban DOC-certified wine. A second location is in the Corso di Porta Nuova.

3 PANDENUS

5 traditional
PASTRY SHOPS

6 **PASTICCERIA CUCCHI**
Corso Genova 1
Sant'Ambrogio ④
+39 02 8940 9793
pasticceriacucchi.it

One of those rare places where you feel as if time has stopped, especially on Sunday mornings at breakfast, when people at the outdoor tables browse the newspapers and the waiters take their orders. Coffee and cappuccinos are served with delicious croissants. A traditional pastry shop that produces its own artisanal *panettone*.

7 **MARCHESI 1824**
Via S. Maria alla Porta 11-A
5vie ②
+39 02 862 770
pasticceria marchesi.com

The interiors date from the early 20th century, with low-coffered ceilings, mirrors and art deco lamps. Inside, the smell of coffee and custard cream pastries wafts towards you. Do taste their rice puddings. Marchesi was acquired by the Prada Group a few years ago, and opened other branches, in Via Monte Napoleone and in Galleria Vittorio Emanuele II.

8 **SANT AMBROEUS**

Corso Matteotti 7
Duomo-San Babila ②
+39 02 7600 0540
*santambroeus
milano.com*

The place to stop after shopping in the quadrilateral, aka Milan's fashion district, and a historic venue. Sitting at its tables can be expensive. A coffee at the counter costs much less (in Italy you'll pay 1 to 1,20 euro on average). Do try their famous grilled sandwich with *provola* and anchovies.

9 **GIOVANNI GALLI**

Corso di Porta
Romana 2
Porta Romana ②
+39 02 8645 3112
giovannigalli.com

The wooden counter and display cases were taken from their first location at Porta Romana, which was established in 1912 and destroyed during the WWII bombings. At the time, the pastry shop was a supplier to the Royal House of Savoy. They opened a second shop in Via Victor Hugo, which is their busiest branch nowadays. Famous for its candied chocolate-covered chestnuts, and the *boeri* chocolates.

10 **PASTICCERIA SISSI**

Piazza Risorgimento 6
East ⑥
+39 02 7601 4664

A place that is bound to become 'historic'. Not for its adorable tiny courtyard garden, where you can sometimes find yourself alone on weekdays, while you drink a coffee and read the newspaper, but for its baked goods, creams and chocolate cakes. Peek in the open workshop if you want to steal some trade secrets. Alternatively, just enjoy the relaxed atmosphere.

5
FOOD MARKETS
and more

---

11 PECK 1883
Via Spadari 9
5vie ②
+39 02 8023 161
peck.it

Its history commences in 1883 when a butcher from Prague opened a 'German-style' meat and sausage shop in the city. Over the years it expanded, a deli was added and it became the city's most famous food temple. Their hampers are a must-have for the holidays, like their Olivier salad. There is also a wine shop in the cellar.

11 PECK 1883

12 **MERCATO COMUNALE WAGNER**
Piazza Riccardo Wagner
West ⑧
mercatocomunale wagner.com

The Suigo family's fish stand has been here since the market opened in 1929. The Dibenedetto butchery sells fine Piedmontese meats and you can buy cheese from the Lettieri stall. Try before you buy. Do not forget Ceba delicatessen. Great for people watching and to spot VIPs.

13 **MERCATO DEL SUFFRAGIO**
Piazza Santa Maria del Suffragio 2
East ⑥
+39 02 5518 4461

This small 'covered market with a kitchen', in the Porta Vittoria area, is home to the Longoni bakery, which sells naturally leavened bread and pizzas, a fruit and vegetable shop that prepares vegetarian dishes, and a fishmonger. Perfect for a quick dinner albeit not cheap.

14 **SLOW FOOD MERCATO DELLA TERRA**
AT: LA FABBRICA DEL VAPORE
Via Giulio Cesare Procaccini 4
North-West ⑩
mercatidellaterra.com

Over 40 growers from Rural Park South Milan – one of the largest peri-urban parks in Europe, with 47.000 hectares of land – sell their wares here. Their open-air stalls are simply overflowing with produce, rice, honey, and many Slow Food Presidia products. Open on the first and third Saturday of the month (9 am – 2 pm).

15 **MERCATO ISOLA**
Piazzale Lagosta 7
Isola ⑩
mercatoisola.it

The historic 1950s covered market in Piazzale Lagosta has been given a makeover, in keeping with the neighbourhood's new vibe. Inside you'll find a selection of gourmet artisans and carefully chosen producers, surrounded by large terraces, big glass windows and the latest technology.

5 places to
FEEL AT HOME

---

16 **RISO E LATTE**
   Via Camperio 6
   5vie ②
   +39 02 3983 1040
   risoelatte.com

A place to go to when you miss home: not yours that is, but your auntie's. Where everything has remained unchanged since your childhood, with pastel tables and chairs, 1960s-style plateware and a jukebox that plays familiar old tunes. Where they cook the food of your youth.

17 **DABASS**
   Via Piacenza 13
   Porta Romana ②
   +39 349 356 5436

A play on the Milanese word for 'downstairs'. Casa Sartorio, designed by architect Provasi, is located inside this 'triangular' building that dates from 1909. Cocktails, mixed by Robi Tardelli, are paired with food here. With 20th-century design furniture, mismatched dinnerware, in a cosy 'home' away from home.

18 TORRE DI PISA

Via Fiori Chiari 21/5
Brera-Corso
Garibaldi ①
+39 02 874 877
trattoriatorredipisa.it

Dark wooden furniture, white tablecloths on the tables, and paintings and bottles everywhere you look. This traditional *trattoria,* which is tucked away in Milan's old town, has been popular with artists, intellectuals and businessmen since the sixties. A delectable selection of Tuscan food awaits, including crostini, homemade ravioli and entrecote alla 'Vaj' (with rosemary and chilli flakes).

19 PORTINERIA 14

Via Ettore Troilo 14
South-West ⑨
+39 02 8352 1290

A bar that doubles as a service centre, like a conciergerie for the neighbourhood, with boxes where you can leave an extra set of keys, a place where they mind your dog for ten minutes, where you can find a list of craftsmen (plumbers, electricians, painters) and where you can enjoy a drink!

20 LA CUCINA ITALIANA SCHOOL

Piazzale Cadorna 5
ENTRANCE:
Via San Nicolao 7
Cairoli-Castello ③
+39 02 4974 8004
scuola.lacucina italiana.it

Founded in 1929, *La Cucina Italiana* is the magazine – with a kitchen in the newsroom – that all our mothers have been buying for many years. They also have an increasingly popular cooking school. Courses are often organised in the morning and end just in time for lunchtime. You eat what you cooked together, like at a friend's house.

5 gourmet
PIZZA PLACES
to discover

---

21 **BERBERÈ**
Via Sebenico 21
Isola ⑩
+39 02 3670 7820
berberepizza.it

Housed in the historic Circolo Filippo Sassetti, which was founded in 1911 as a building cooperative, this place has deliberately maintained the appearance of a Milanese restaurant of the forties or fifties. The pizza dough is made from semi-wholemeal organic flour. Here pizzas are served cut into slices, so you can share.

22 **LIEVITO MADRE AL DUOMO**
Largo Corsia
dei Servi 11
(Corso Vittorio
Emanuele)
Duomo-San Babila ②
sorbillo.it

They don't take reservations, so muster all your patience and, on cold winter days, try other places in the area, because they only bake 400 pizzas every evening. The restaurant is owned by Gino Sorbillo, who also operates the popular place on the waterfront in Naples. If you fail to get a table the first time, try again.

23 **CROSTA**
Via Felice Bellotti 12
East ⑥
+39 02 3824 8570
crosta.eu

A cross between a bakery and a pizzeria, Crosta (crust) combines the art of bread making by Giovanni Mineo and the skill of Simone Lombardi. Here you will find bread with ancient grains and sourdough and classic or contemporary pizzas with very special ingredients.

24 PIZ

Via Torino 34
5vie ②
+39 02 8645 3482

Pasquale Pometto opened his Piz in the alley leading to Cinema Centrale. Here you can eat a real Neapolitan pizza, in a noisy, boisterous setting, which is very different from the overly sophisticated restaurants of his competitors. No reservations possible. Try his interpretation of the 'Marinara'.

25 MARGHE

Via Cadore 26
Porta Romana ②
+39 02 5411 8711
lnx.marghepizza.com

Locally produced buffalo mozzarella, Piennolo del Vesuvio tomatoes, fresh basil, organic extra virgin olive oil. Marghe, the discovery of the year, combines fresh ingredients with a long proving process. The menu features a short list of excellent choices as well as speciality pizzas and vegan options. A second location is in Via Plinio.

21 BERBERÈ

28 UN POSTO A MILANO

5 places with a
GARDEN

---

26 RATANÀ

Via Gaetano de
Castillia 28
Isola ⑩
+39 02 8712 8855
ratana.it

In a small building, dwarfed by the skyscrapers of Porta Nuova, chef Cesare Battisti prepares dishes that 'express the soul of Milan', sourcing his raw material from local producers. The risottos and meats are excellent. His partner and sommelier Federica Fabi is in charge of the front of house. Games for children in the garden.

27 U BARBA

Via Pier Candido
Decembrio 33
South-East ⑦
+39 02 4548 7032
ubarba.it

A *bocce* club which has become a Genovese tavern. The food is very basic here, and includes *trofie* (short, twisted pasta) with pesto, *pansotti* (stuffed pasta) with walnut sauce, and cheese-stuffed focaccia. You can enjoy their cuisine, that reminds the Milanese of weekends by the sea, at a communal table. Or outdoors, near the *bocce* court. Also open for lunch on weekends.

28 UN POSTO A MILANO

Via Privata
Cuccagna 2
Porta Romana ②
+39 02 5457 785
unpostoamilano.it

An 18th-century farmhouse, with two courtyards and a large garden with fruit trees in the heart of Milan, is home to a locally grown cooking project and a guesthouse, with four rooms that have been furnished in a simple and natural style. A place that combines a sustainable lifestyle, healthy food and urban agriculture.

29 ERBA BRUSCA

Alzaia Naviglio
Pavese 286
South-West ⑨
+39 02 8738 0711
erbabrusca.it

A garden tucked away at the end of the Naviglio, where the city becomes the countryside. With a table, under a pergola on hot, sunny days, where you can enjoy the cooking of Alice Delcourt, which is as fragrant as the vegetables and the greens from her garden. After eating, you can take one of the bikes for a spin around the area.

30 AL CORTILE

Via Giovenale 7
South-East ⑦
+39 02 8909 3079
alcortile.com

In this slightly secluded courtyard, near the Fonderie Milanesi, you feel as if you've left the city for the countryside. Stop at the red house for an aperitivo with friends. Also a perfect place for a dinner on the terrace.

5 places to enjoy
ICE CREAM

---

31 GELATO GIUSTO
Via San Gregorio 17
Porta Venezia ⑤
+39 02 2951 0284
gelatogiusto.it

Young Vittoria Bortolazzo graduated from Cordon Bleu after which she worked at Ladurée, Lenôtre and the École Valrhona. Here she creates 'gourmet' ice creams, i.e., special combinations, with no added flavours, colourings or preservatives. The fresh basil ice cream is a popular summer choice, *panettone* is perfect for winter.

32 PAVÉ GELATI & GRANITE
Via Cesare Battisti 21
Porta Romana ②
+39 02 9438 3619
pavemilano.com

The team at Pavé has a growing fanbase, making the bakery at Via Casati 27 a must (and the *NYTimes* agrees). They also won Three Cones from food mag *Gambero Rosso* for their ice creams. Try bread and butter 160 (as in 160 grams of apricots for 100 grams of jam), of course, named after their iconic brioche.

33 GELATERIA PAGANELLI
Via Adda 3
North-East ⑤
+39 02 6702 751

Three Cones also for Francesco Paganelli's ice cream as he continues to create innovative flavours. Intrepid foodies should try his olive oil ice cream, the basil cream or the classic salted pistachio. His Sicilian granitas are equally delicious.

34 ARTICO GELATERIA TRADIZIONALE

Via Porro
Lambertenghi 15
Isola ⑩
+39 02 4549 4698
articogelateria.com

A must-visit in Isola. During the last week of September, they organise a 'chocolate show', with 32 different types of chocolate ice cream, from the classics (milk chocolate or *gianduia*) to more sophisticated ones with tobacco, rum or Barolo. Maurizio Poloni has also founded the Artico Ice Cream School, if you want to learn more about the art of ice-cream making.

35 GUSTO 17

Via Savona 17
Porta Genova ⑨
+39 02 3981 1835
gusto17.com

The tiny space overlooking Via Savona is easy to miss but it would be a shame if you did. This 'agro-ice-cream parlour' only uses Italian ingredients, fresh fruit, and organic milk and cream. Try the buffalo ricotta cream, the matcha tea tiramisu or the *babà*, and the ice-cream-filled Sicilian brioche.

31 GELATO GIUSTO

5
STREET FOOD
places you can't afford to miss

---

36 **MANUELINA**
Via Santa
Radegonda 10
Duomo-San Babila ②
+39 02 8852 297
*manuelina
focacceria.it/milano*

In Liguria, no seaside evening would be complete without a cheese-stuffed focaccia from Recco, and Manuelina is the place to eat it in Milan. They opened a few years ago and since then it has become the perfect place to (temporarily) appease any pangs of culinary (holiday) nostalgia.

37 **SCIATT À PORTER**
Viale Monte
Grappa 18
North-West ⑩
+39 02 6347 0524
sciattaporter.it

Dedicated to street food, from the nearby Valtellina region – a basket full of cheese, cured and salted meats and great wines – you can now sample these flavours in Porta Nuova, including *sciatt*, buckwheat fritters with Casera cheese and *pizzoccheri* with Savoy cabbage and potatoes (to be eaten while sitting down).

38 **AL POLITICO**
Piazza Castello 5
Cairoli-Castello ③

The sandwiches are all named after politicians. But does the generous filling fit their character? Who cares about politics, here it's all about the food! Very popular with journalists who work for the nearby newspapers.

39 RAVIOLERIA SARPI

Via Paolo Sarpi 27
Chinatown ⑩
+39 331 8870 596

Gather your patience and join the queue at this small dumpling bar in Chinatown. Everything is made to order in the open kitchen, from the crepes, which also come in a veggie version, to the famous ravioli with beef or pork meat from the nearby Sirtori butcher shop, the restaurant's partner. They only use the best ingredients here.

40 MACELLERIA POPOLARE CON CUCINA

Piazza XXIV Maggio 4
Navigli ⑨
+39 02 3946 8368
mangiaridistrada.com

Arrosticini, scottadito, bombette (meat skewers) and other local specialities prepared with organic meat. Eat them at the renovated Municipal Market in Piazza XXIV Maggio, at the Darsena. It is both a butcher's shop and a delicatessen. They also own a bakery and cheese shop in the same market.

39 RAVIOLERIA SARPI

5
TRATTORIAS
to experience authentic cuisine

---

41 **TRATTORIA MADONNINA**
Via Gentilino 6
South-East ⑦
+39 02 8940 9089

Returning to this inn from the early 1900s, with its authentic popular atmosphere, is always a pleasure. Antique interior and a small terrace outside. The menu is reassuring, with simple dishes and main courses of meat, which is boiled, stewed, and braised, as well as the typical veal Milanese, of course.

42 **MASUELLI S. MARCO 1921**
Viale Umbria 80
Porta Romana ②
+39 02 5518 4138
masuellitrattoria.com

The sight of white tablecloths, 1930s chandeliers by Venini – designed by Giò Ponti – and Thonet chairs from the 1920s has been a familiar one for customers of this 'historic shop' for three generations. Just like the flavours of Lombardic-Piedmontese cuisine that chef Max Masuelli reinvents here, with a contemporary twist. Try the bone-in veal Milanese.

43 ORMA BRUNA

Via Montevideo 4
Porta Genova ⑨
+39 389 607 8866
ormabruna.com

This is a modern *trattoria* where the dishes are inspired by the tradition of central Italy, more specifically from the regions of Le Marche and Abruzzo, but with a contemporary twist and with great respect for ingredients and preparation. Chef Achille Esposito is young and talented, and the location has a simple, almost minimal look, with lots thought given to the interior design. Try the Milano-Abruzzo risotto.

44 TRIPPA

Via Giorgio Vasari 1
Porta Romana ②
+39 327 668 7908
trippamilano.it

Founded by Diego Rossi – who previously worked in the kitchens of Norbert Niederkofler and Alfio Ghezzi, who have 3 and 2 Michelin stars respectively – serving a *neo-trattoria* cuisine. The two rooms are welcoming, from the counter you can see the kitchen and the chef's naughty (and slightly hipstery) moustache.

45 OSTERIA NOVELLI

Via Padova 344
North-East ⑥
+39 02 2720 7769

A real institution (since 1927), this *osteria* is situated on the city's fringe, at one end of Via Padova, the multicultural heart of Milan. An old-fashioned *trattoria* with wood panelling, chequered tablecloths, that serves simple Lombardy fare. Gianni Versace famously used the restaurant as a backdrop for a photo shoot.

41 TRATTORIA MADONNINA

5
REGIONAL CUISINE
restaurants

---

46 TOSCANINO MILANO RISTORANTE E BOTTEGA
Via Melzo /
Via Lambro
Porta Venezia ⑤
+39 02 7428 1354
toscanino.com

The brainchild of Simone Arnetoli, a Florentine, who has brought together the most important wine and food producers and artisans in Tuscany to create an exclusive stockpile of specialities and excellence. All served in a restaurant that makes you feel as if you've just stepped into a Tuscan farmhouse, where everything smells like freshly baked bread.

47 FELICE A TESTACCIO
Via del Torchio 4
Sant'Ambrogio ④
+39 02 8050 6690
feliceatestaccio.it

Founded in a suburb of Rome, where it was renowned for its traditional dishes, it has since burst onto the Milan restaurant scene. Giulia, the third generation of the family and the granddaughter of Felice, the restaurant's founder, is the chef here. This contemporary restaurant, which never forgets its past, serves excellent pasta with cheese and pepper and many other specialities.

48 OLIO-CUCINA FRESCA

Piazzale Lavater 1
Porta Venezia ⑤
+39 02 2052 0503
olioristorante.com

A restaurant where everything is made in Puglia, starting with the extra virgin olive oil, which chef Michele Cobuzzi uses in all of his dishes, and which he combines with Slow Food products, that are cooked in ways so the flavours are not altered. Limited space but they do add some outdoor tables in the summertime.

49 GUSTO PARMIGIANO

Via della Moscova 24
Brera-Corso
Garibaldi ①
+39 02 3651 8884
gustoparmigiano.it

Shop and bistro where everything revolves around *Parmigiano-Reggiano*, which is made with the milk of different breeds of cows – in the plains, hills and mountains – and with different ripening stages. Also serves traditional Emilian cured meats and has a large wine cellar. Chef Federico d'Amato's menu combines between tradition, modernity and... *Parmigiano-Reggiano*. Excellent hot food with aperitivo.

50 AMPÈRE57

Via Ampère 57
East ⑥
+39 02 3652 1125
ristorante
ampere57.com

Amazing Sardinian cuisine, with lots of fish and a wine cellar with local wines. The desserts, including the amaretto biscuits and the *seadas*, filled with cheese and chestnut honey, are simply irresistible. You can eat outside in the summertime.

5 real
VEGETARIAN
places

---

51 JOIA
**Via Panfilo
Castaldi 18
Porta Venezia ⑤
+39 02 2952 2124
*joia.it***

The first meat-free restaurant, serving 'vegetarian haute cuisine', to receive a Michelin star twenty years ago. Pietro Leemann, the chef and owner, has continued to apply this same philosophy that he is happy to share with customers. For lunch you can choose the unique Piatto Quadro (Square Dish).

52 RADICETONDA
**Via Spallanzani 16
Porta Venezia ⑤
+39 02 3673 7924**

**Piazza Buozzi 5
South-East ⑦
+39 02 3673 6669
*radicetonda.it***

A selection of excellent vegan, organic food at the counter, where you'll find dishes with grains, legumes and vegetables, as well as soups. A radical chic atmosphere, with a communal table and outdoor terrace, in the pedestrian area. On sunny days, order takeout and eat in the nearby Indro Montanelli gardens at Porta Venezia.

53 GHEA
**Via Valenza 5
Porta Genova ⑨
+39 02 5811 0980
*gheavegetariano.it***

Ghea is not just a meat-free restaurant. This 'vegetarian laboratory' offers natural and vegan cuisine with special respect for nature and the fragile balance of the ecosystem. They pay great attention to raw, seasonal ingredients and flavours.

54 FLOWER BURGER

**Viale Vittorio
Veneto 10
Porta Venezia** ⑤
+39 02 3962 8381

**Via Tortona 12
Porta Genova** ⑨
+39 02 3946 9907
flowerburger.it

An offshoot of the gourmet burger era, Flower Burger serves colourful and vegetarian versions of this popular dish, including Tofungo, the Flower Burger and Cheesy Cecio. The bread is homemade with turmeric, 7 grains or black with charcoal. Toppings include hummus and caramelised onions. Tables are often shared.

55 LA VECCHIA LATTERIA MILANO

**Via dell'Unione 6
Duomo-San Babila** ②
+39 02 874 401

After WWII, *latterie* were shops with a few tables serving a few simple dishes, such as poached eggs and vegetables. People ate together, often sharing tables. The atmosphere has remained the same since then, the cuisine is vegetarian, but the prices are contemporary. Try the sample platter *(Misto Forno)*.

54 FLOWER BURGER

5

SOCIAL DINING SPOTS

---

56 **ROB DE MATT**
AT: L'AMICO CHARLY
Via Enrico Annibale
Butti 18
North-West ⑩
+39 388 446 1762
robdematt.org

A good *trattoria,* with its own vegetable garden, working with organic ingredients, mindful of the short supply chain and respectful of sustainability (also in the tab). Rob de Matt is located in the suburban area of Dergano and was created to promote the social and working inclusion of people with mental disabilities.

57 **BISTRŌLINDA**
AT: TEATRO ELFO PUCCINI
Corso Buenos
Aires 33
Porta Venezia ⑤
+39 02 3660 1805
olinda.org

The bistro of the Elfo Puccini Theatre has a dozen small tables and a few very well-made dishes on the menu, all originating in the Italian tradition, which will also satisfy the taste buds of vegetarian customers. Excellent cakes. Managed by a cooperative that provides employment for people in need.

58 INGALERA

AT: PRISON OF BOLLATE
Via Cristina
Belgioioso 120
North-West ⑩
+39 334 3081 189
ingalera.it

This place claims to be the only Italian restaurant in a prison, the correctional facility of Bollate, that is open to the public. The inmates work here, supervised by a professional chef and a maître d', serving an à la carte menu at lunch and dinner and a tasting menu, with very captivating dishes. Book in advance.

59 RAB

Corso San
Gottardo 41
South-West ⑨
+39 02 8352 0869
spaziorab.it

At Rab, a literary cafe, you can enjoy breakfast, a snack, or lunch. You can study or work at the co-working stations. Read or participate in the theatre and art workshops. At night, stop for an aperitivo and maybe see an exhibition. People with learning disabilities work here.

60 REFETTORIO AMBROSIANO

Piazza Greco 11
North-West ⑩
+39 02 760 371
refettorioambrosiano.it

The Modena-based three-star chef Massimo Bottura gave a strong boost to Refettorio Ambrosiano. He involved artists and designers – and many chef friends – in this restaurant, which is run by a charitable organisation called Caritas, to help the needy. A beautiful project, which he subsequently also exported to Rio de Janeiro, London and Paris.

5 places to sample
CONTEMPORARY ASIAN CUISINE

61 **WICKY'S WICUISINE**
Corso Italia 6
Porta Romana ②
+39 02 8909 3781
wicuisine.it

A restaurant you can't afford to miss. If you choose a 'front-row' seat, at the counter with Wicky Priyan, you can watch the master chef prepare a menu of his own inspiration, while you look on. Although he is of Sinhalese origin, he lived in Japan for several years, learning the local techniques and culture. The menu also features 'Milanese' sushi with saffron rice.

62 **BON WEI**
Via Castelvetro 16-18
North-West ⑩
+39 02 341 308
bon-wei.it

A restaurant where they serve Chinese regional haute cuisine, with fresh products and high-quality ingredients combined in surprising dishes. The restaurant is modern, very comfortable, with special lighting and red artwork on the walls. Try the Peking duck or the sautéed lobster with ginger.

63 IYO

Via Piero della
Francesca 74
North-West ⑩
+39 02 4547 6898
iyo.it

The Japanese restaurant of the Chinese Liu family has a Michelin star. Michele Biassoni works in the open kitchen, while the sushi counter is in the skilful hands of Masaki Okada, a master at preparing raw dishes. IYO serves contemporary cuisine.

64 RISTORANTE TOKUYOSHI

Via San Calocero 3
Sant'Ambrogio ④
+39 02 8425 4626
ristorante
tokuyoshi.com

Perhaps telling you that he was a sous-chef of Massimo Bottura when the Osteria Francescana earned its second and then third Michelin star is sufficient. But Yoji Tokuyoshi has since opened his own restaurant, where you can taste his own signature 'Italian fusion cuisine'.

65 CITTAMANI

Piazza Carlo
Mirabello 5
Brera-Corso
Garibaldi ①
+39 02 3824 0935
cittamani.com

The arrival of Ritu Dalmia, originally from Marwar, a region in Northern India, was more than eagerly awaited. The chef, who is very famous in her country, chose the Brera area to open Cittamani. Shivanjali Shankar is in charge here, serving contemporary Indian cuisine working with Italian ingredients.

5
MASTERS OF
ITALIAN CUISINE

---

66 **SPAZIO NIKO ROMITO MILANO**
AT: GALLERIA VITTORIO EMANUELE II, 4TH FLOOR
Piazza del Duomo 1
Duomo-San Babila ②
+39 02 878 400
spazionikoromito.com/ristorante

Originally established as a place to train the students of Accademia Niko Romito, the cooking school of the three-star chef from Abruzzo, inside Mercato del Duomo. Over the years it has evolved, although it is still one of the most interesting spots in the city, and one of the most relaxing places in the centre, with a view of the Duomo's steeples. The chef also runs Ristorante Niko Romito at the Bulgari Hotel in Milan, where he reinterprets classic Italian dishes with a contemporary twist.

67 **FILIPPO LA MANTIA – OSTE & CUOCO**
AT: MERCATO CENTRALE MILANO
Via Giovanni Battista Sammartini 2
North-East ⑤
+39 02 3792 8410
mercatocentrale.it/milano/artigiani/il-ristorante-filippo-la-mantia-oste-e-cuoco

Host, chef and artisan (as he likes to call himself) Filippo La Mantia has started an eighty-seat adventure in the Mercato Centrale (at the Central Station). His cuisine embodies the traditions, flavours and colours of Sicily, his homeland, but "without garlic, onion, leeks or shallots", as his admirers well know.

68 SETA – ANTONIO GUIDA

AT: HOTEL MANDARIN ORIENTAL
Via Andegari 9
Brera-Corso
Garibaldi ①
+39 02 8731 8897
mandarinoriental.com

He was awarded two Michelin stars in just two years at the Mandarin. His cuisine has been said to have 'neat, clear and never indecisive flavours'. One of his recipes, rice with butter, sage, cheese, vegetables, and raspberry powder, is a contemporary reinterpretation of a typical dish from Lombardy.

69 LUME – LUIGI TAGLIENTI

Via Giacomo Watt 37
South-West ⑨
+39 02 8088 8624
lumemilano.com

Luigi Taglienti tries to source the best raw materials, while always paying attention to the connection with terroir. In addition to the interior, with its designer furnishings, you should also check out L'Orto di Lume in summertime, another all-white space, where you can smell the tomato plants and the aromatic herbs.

70 CRACCO IN GALLERIA

AT: GALLERIA VITTORIO EMANUELE II
Piazza del Duomo 1
Duomo-San Babila ②
+39 02 876 774
ristorantecracco.it

Frescos, stucco, hand-painted wallpaper, large windows facing the Octagon and antique furniture, pointing to an architectural legacy spanning from the second half of the 1800s to Giò Ponti. Have dinner in Carlo Cracco's gourmet restaurant or treat yourself to coffee and a croissant (prepared by the pastry chef Marco Pedron) on the ground floor or at the outdoor tables. Also a great after-theatre spot.

The 5 best
AFTER OPERA
places

---

71 JAMAICA BAR
Via Brera 32
Brera-Corso
Garibaldi ①
+39 02 876 723
jamaicabar.it

Everything at this place, which opened in the early 20th century, refers to the people who have hung out here over the years, with artists and writers – including Quasimodo and Ungaretti, painters like Lucio Fontana and the Nobel Prize laureate Dario Fo, as well as professors and students from the nearby Academy of Brera.

72 LA LIBERA
Via Palermo 21
Brera-Corso
Garibaldi ①
+39 02 8053 603
lalibera.it

The Brera district is just behind La Scala. After the performance pop into this typical Milanese-style *trattoria*, with its original counter, wood panelling, and tables that are close to each other. The cuisine is definitely Milanese: do try the typical *Riso al salto* (fried rice cakes) and the meat dishes.

73 ROSY E GABRIELE 1
Via Sirtori 26
Porta Venezia ⑤
+39 02 2952 5930

Open until late, which is why you'll often see actors and comedians, models and photographers there, after a long day on set. A simple place, with a crowd-pleasing menu, fresh fish and good pizza. A spot where, even if you're alone, you never feel out of place.

74 A SANTA LUCIA

**Via San Pietro
all'Orto 3
Duomo-San Babila** ②
+39 02 7602 3155
asantalucia.it

Traditionally a favourite place to stop for the after-theatre crowd. Customers at its first location in Via d'Agnello included d'Annunzio, Mascagni, Edoardo de Filippo, and Totò. The owners took the original furnishings and historic sign with them to the current location, just a few metres up the street. Famous guests there include Sinatra, Liza Minelli and Maria Callas, whose pictures are all on the walls.

75 IL FOYER

**Via Filodrammatici 2
Duomo-San Babila** ②
+39 02 7209 4338
gualtieromarchesi.it

Gualtiero Marchesi, the founder of Italian modern cuisine and the 'father' of almost all the Milanese starred chefs, died in 2017. Fortunately we can still enjoy his legacy at his restaurant, near La Scala, which continues to be a must-stop for many foodies. Gold leaf saffron risotto was his signature dish.

71 JAMAICA BAR

5

HEALTHY & ORGANIC

places

---

76 CONTRADA GOVINDA
Via Valpetrosa 5
5Vie ②
+39 02 4954 2241
contradagovinda.com

A former canteen of the Hare Krishna society and one of the first vegetarian restaurants in Milan. Davide Longoni, one of Milan's most renowned bakers, has opened a bakery in Casa dei Grifi (a 14th-century building) as well as a small vegetarian restaurant that serves inventive vegetarian fare that you can wash down with non-alcoholic drinks and mocktails.

77 CASCINA NASCOSTA
AT: PARCO SEMPIONEC
Cairoli-Castello ③
+39 340 675 5196
cascinanascosta.org

The building, which looks like a Lombardy farmhouse with its typical courtyard, is tucked away between two embankments in Parco Sempione. Here they promote (food) sustainability in various ways. Head to the Latteria (Dairy) where you can sample dishes that are suited to most dietary requirements, made from healthy, seasonal ingredients sourced from the surrounding countryside.

78 BIOESSERÍ

Via Fatebenefratelli 2
Brera-Corso
Garibaldi ①
+39 02 8907 1052
bioesseri.it

Identità Golose, the Haute Cuisine congress, applauded the quality of the cuisine at this place, which was founded by two Sicilian brothers, preparing organic dishes in a contemporary setting. Bioesserí is open from breakfast till dinner, with a corner dedicated to gastronomic shopping. The pizza is definitely worth trying.

79 NABI-NATURA BIOLOGICA

Via Cadore 41
Porta Romana ②
+39 02 3674 0247
naturabiologica.net/nabi

A light cuisine, with very little dressing, so the ingredients, many of which are plant-based, are the stars of the show. Croissants filled to order for breakfast, fresh cakes for tea time, and a main course with four different options. At dinnertime, from Wednesday till Sunday, NaBi reopens as the veggie SoloBurgher.

80 THAT'S VAPORE

Via Michelangelo
Buonarroti 3
West ⑧
+39 02 4351 1568
thatsvapore.it

That's Vapore has branches all over the city, largely because it caters to the Milanese population's need to always be light and fit, thanks to steam cooking. A selection of healthy and tasty fish or meat and vegetables, combined with juices, smoothies and fresh fruit. Deliveries possible.

5

HEALTHY DELIVERY

services you may enjoy

81 **NANIE**
nanie.com

Delivered to you by e-vehicle, wrapped in eco-friendly packaging and made to order with products selected by taste experts and artisans. The menu changes often, but some dishes never get old, such as the megahummus with Tuscan black chickpeas, fennel, cauliflower and a Tuscan kale salad, with sourdough bread toast.

82 **MUGS AND CO.**
Via Emilio Morosini 4
East ⑥
+39 02 8738 3354
mugsandco.eu

While its appearance might make you think of New York, this cafe and bakery definitely has a Neapolitan heart. The menu offers a good selection of vegan options – lactose-free but equally tasty – which can also be delivered directly to your home or office, and with 100% compostable packaging. They are also quite famous for brunch, held here every day of the week. Excellent homemade cakes.

83 DIET TO GO

+39 02 8715 9091
diet-to-go.com

A delivery service for those who want to go on a diet but who are not interested in cooking and counting calories. Select a daily or weekly plan, with a Mediterranean, vegetarian or detox menu.
All you need for the day is delivered in a cooler, i.e. breakfast, lunch, a snack and dinner.

84 ORTICELLO

Viale Monte Nero 22
Porta Romana ②
+39 02 8354 9655
orticellotakeaway.it

Developed to offer a healthy and light menu, the project of Cristina Chiusano, a chef of Piedmontese origin, and Alessandra Schatzinger offers take-out and gourmet delivery, using only the best ingredients. Simple yet special food, which you can sample anywhere you wish, at home and at the office.

85 CORTILIA

+39 02 8719 7503
cortilia.it

Cortilia will deliver a crate of fresh and organic products anywhere you want, even once only, without a subscription. Choose between fruits and vegetables or a mix of both on their website, and add bread, cheese, honey, preserves and much more. All sourced from local producers.

BAR LUCE

60 PLACES TO GO
FOR A DRINK

———

The 5 best places for
APERITIVO

---

86 FRIDA
Via A. Pollaiuolo 3
Isola ⑩
+39 02 680 260
fridaisola.it

A place with a long-standing history, in the Isola neighbourhood, with a courtyard full of tables. In the summertime it is buzzing with people. An informal setting, affordable prices and plenty of beer, including several Italian brands. Start with some nibbles for aperitivo and spend the night chatting and listening to good music.

86 FRIDA

87 MAG CAFÈ

Ripa di Porta Ticinese 43
Navigli ⑨
+39 02 3956 2875

A Bohemian atmosphere, with a wooden counter and antique furniture. A well-known address for quality mixed drinks and a list of cocktails that changes seasonally. Owned by Flavio Angiolillo and Marco Russo who also own the 1930 and BackDoor43.

88 FONDERIE MILANESI

Via Giovenale 7
South-East ⑦
+39 02 3652 7913
fonderiemilanesi.it

Go down a private road and you'll suddenly find yourself in an inner courtyard, which becomes a charming and romantic place in the evening. But the atmosphere is relaxed, like the people at this bar: young people (from the nearby Bocconi University), who enjoy tucking into the moreish portions of pasta and focaccia at a large wooden table.

89 CAFÉ GORILLE

Via G. de Castillia 20
Isola ⑩
+39 02 6887 627
cafegorille.it

Once upon a time there used to be artists' studios and craftsmen's workshops on these premises, which opened in 1882. Today that relaxed atmosphere is still very much retained in a bistro with informal furnishings and style, and which is run by a group of friends. Open from morning till evening.

90 PANIFICIO DAVIDE LONGONI

Via G. Tiraboschi 19
Porta Romana ②
+39 02 9163 8069
davidelongonipane.com

While this may be slightly off the beaten track, it is still fashionable. The shop with its little garden is a popular haunt for connoisseurs when the clock strikes five. Of bread connoisseurs of course. At Longoni, all the bread is sourdough, made from organic flour and ancient grains.

5 cool
BARS IN MUSEUMS

---

91 LÙBAR
AT: VILLA REALE GAM
Via Palestro 16
Porta Venezia ①
+39 02 8352 7769
lubar.it

Today the former orangerie of Villa Reale is a splendid winter garden, with large windows overlooking the greenery. The tables also occupy part of the southern portico, through which the horses once entered. The atmosphere is laidback, like in the park where there's an area designed for children.

92 BAR LUCE
AT: FONDAZIONE PRADA
Largo Isarco 2
South-East ⑦
+39 02 5666 2611
fondazioneprada.org

When this place opened it became the hipsters' new favourite hang-out, from breakfast till evening. The best moment to enjoy the bar, which was designed by Wes Anderson, who won an Oscar for *The Grand Budapest Hotel*, is on weekdays, without the chaos of the weekend.

93 CAFFÈ FERNANDA
AT: PINACOTECA DI BRERA
Via Brera 28
Brera-Corso
Garibaldi ①
+39 345 050 4846
caffefernanda.com

The beautiful bar of the Pinacoteca di Brera, with its large wooden counter, is open all day and also has some tables on the terrace. For their menu they can count on advice from Filippo La Mantia, a well-known Sicilian chef (who has a restaurant that carries his name, in Piazza Risorgimento).

94 VÒCE AIMO E NADIA
AT: GALLERIE D'ITALIA
Piazza della Scala 6
Duomo-San Babila ②
+39 02 4070 1935
voceaimoenadia.com

A cafe, a restaurant, and a bookshop: this ambitious project aims at bringing food, culture, and art together in one place. The cafe is always open; at lunchtime it offers a variety of salads with homemade focaccias, made with stone-ground flour from ancient grains. Then there is the gourmet restaurant, where Fabio Pisani and Alessandro Negrini, present their interpretation of Italian cuisine.

95 GIACOMO CAFFÈ
AT: PALAZZO REALE
Piazza del Duomo 12
Duomo-San Babila ②
+39 02 8909 6698
giacomocaffe.com

One of the stars of the 'Giacomo' constellation, which includes a restaurant in the nearby Arengario and an enclave in Via Sottocorno with a bistro, pastry shop and bar-tobacco shop. The cafe of Palazzo Reale also has a pleasant courtyard and a mezzanine where you can browse old and recent exhibition catalogues.

91 LÙBAR

The 5 best
WINE BARS

---

96 **BICERÌN**
Via Panfilo
Castaldi 24
Porta Venezia ⑤
+39 02 8425 8410
bicerinmilano.com

Silvia, Alberto, and Lorenzo welcome you into their elegant, comfortable living room with antique furniture, where you can enjoy good drinks. A pleasant place to while away the time in the company of friends, with top-class labels and improvised dinners. They often organise wine tastings with small producers and also offer a lunch service.

97 **LA CIECA**
Via Carlo Vittadini 6
South-East ⑦
+39 02 5843 7901
lacieca.it

This wine shop only works with small Italian wineries. Wine by the glass, with a platter of cold cuts or cheese. If you're up for a game, why not go for a 'blind tasting': guess the wine, the vintage and the producer, and you win the bottle as a gift.

98 **CANTINE ISOLA**
Via Paolo Sarpi 30 /
Via Arnolfo di
Cambio 1-A
Chinatown ⑩
+39 02 3315 249
cantineisola.com

There is always a small crowd in the pedestrian area of Chinatown around aperitivo time. Look behind them for the entrance to a historic place, that has become synonymous with good drinking. The wine shop is a hole in the wall, like a 'bookshelf' where bottles have replaced the books.

99 VINO AL VINO

Via Gaspare
Spontini 11
East ⑥
+39 02 2941 4928

Even if you drink by the glass, you can choose from any bottle. The cost is a quarter of the price of the bottle – and if you want a whole bottle and don't finish it, you get to take it home. A simple format, like the furnishings, which display the boxes of bottles, from small vintners, from Italy and other countries.

100 E/N ENOTECA NATURALE

Via Santa Croce 19
Sant'Ambrogio ④
+39 02 8277 0589
enotecanaturale.it

Have a glass of wine in the courtyard and enjoy the beauty of the basilica of Sant'Eustorgio. The place has about 250 types of natural wine, made by small producers. The space belongs to Emergency, an independent and neutral association that ensures care for victims of war, and e/n enoteca naturale contributes by providing traineeships to asylum seekers.

96 BICERIN

5 awesome bars
for a **BEER**

---

101 GHE PENSI M.I.

Piazza Morbegno 2
NoLo ⑤
+39 351 974 4469
ghepensi-mi.it

Surfboards and a super relaxed environment. At Ghe Pensi M.I. (I'll take care of that, in Milanese dialect) you can drink artisanal beer, eat well-stuffed sandwiches or platters. Here you'll feel a distinctly southern influence, and when it comes to food, fun and relaxation, the party's on.

102 LAMBIC ZOON

Via Friuli 46
Porta Romana ②
+39 02 3653 4840
lambiczoon.com

Lambic is a type of beer that is produced in Belgium with spontaneous fermentation, which explains the name. A place for beer connoisseurs, with ten beers on tap. In addition to the 'sour' beers, there are Pilsners, Porters and IPAs from Italian breweries. Order a tasty burger to go with your beer.

103 IMPRONTA BIRRAIA

Via Tucidide 56
East ⑥
+39 02 3707 2071
improntabirraia.com

A brew pub in Ortica, where the Milanese 'mob' used to reign supreme at one time. Located in an early-20th-century building, they serve a selection of craft brews here. Hibu stands out though: an Italian company that produces barley and hops in Lombardy and Basilicata, with over 30 different beers.

104 BIRRIFICIO LA RIBALTA

Via Cevedale 3
North-West ⑲
+39 02 3932 9002
birrificiolaribalta.com

During the warmer months, you feel as if you are light-years away from the city in their courtyard. And in fact you are in the suburbs, in a colourful space, with spartan repurposed furniture. Popular with a young crowd, often with live music. And you get to drink craft beer, right next to where it's produced.

105 BIRRIFICIO LAMBRATE

Via Golgi 60
East ⑥
+39 02 8496 1890
birrificiolambrate.com

These forerunners of the craft beer movement produce unpasteurised and unfiltered beer, with only water, barley malt, hops and yeast. The names are made in Milan: from 'Lambrate', the name of the neighbourhood, to 'Sant'Ambroeus', the city's patron saint and 'Ghisa', which in Milan means traffic policeman. English pub atmosphere with a restaurant.

5
COCKTAIL BARS
you can't afford to miss

—————

106 NOTTINGHAM FOREST
Viale Piave 1
East ⑥
nottingham-forest.com

Its bar counter crossed the ocean, where it previously stood in one of the bars of the Knickerbocker Hotel in New York, a cult place for bartenders. But this tiny place is also a cult place, where Dario Comini, a 21st-century alchemist, weaves his magic. This Italian venue for years has featured prominently on the World's 50 Best Bars list. Enjoy!

107 CINC BRERA
Via Marco Formentini 5
Brera-Corso Garibaldi ①
+39 02 3655 0257
cincbrera.it

Set in a former furniture store in the most evocative area of Milan, this place has a casual atmosphere. While it's open from morning till night, it's worth popping in at aperitif time, for drinks with olives and crisps. You'll only appreciate the list of cocktails by Luca Pirola even more.

108 RITA
Via Angelo Fumagalli 1
Navigli ⑨
+39 02 8372 865

This bar, which is located near the iron bridge, has always gone against the flow, choosing to focus on quality in a very touristy area. The drinks menu will take you on a tour around the world, with the names of the cocktails and the origin of the bottles. The kitchen serves finger food.

109 **BULK**

AT: VIU HOTEL –
MORELLI MILANO
**Via Aristotile
Fioravanti 4**
North-West ⑩
+39 02 8001 0918
morellimilano.it

Bulk is the name of the squat house that stood here before they built the Viu hotel. Its cocktail bar has earned a solid reputation since its opening thanks to the menu by Ivan Patruno who works his magic with the customers from behind the counter. Try the spectacular 'Negroni del Professore'.

110 **RADETZKY**

**Corso Garibaldi 105
Brera-Corso
Garibaldi** ①
+39 02 6572 645
radetzky.it

Although many choose *spritz*, there is an excellent cocktail list to accompany the classic olives, crisps and tiny pizzas, and the slightly gruff service. But then you can't help but pop in here, even if it's almost impossible to find a place at the outdoor tables. Stand with the rest of the patrons, Milan-style.

106 **NOTTINGHAM FOREST**

5 places to discover the
NAVIGLI

---

111 BAR TABACCHI LA DARSENA DA PEPPUCCIO

Via Vigevano 1
Porta Genova ⑨
+39 02 8321 293

Everyone calls it Peppuccio, after its owner, and it looks like any other bar/tobacco shop. Perhaps that is why the radical chic crowd loves this place so much. Well, and then there's also the jazz improv in front of the counter – Peppuccio is also a jazz musician. A popular place with models, students, '*sciure*' (ladies in Milanese), musicians and passers-by in no specific order.

112 ELITA BAR

Via Corsico 5
Porta Genova ⑨
+39 02 3679 8710
elita.it

Never out of style, despite the volatility of the Milanese, who continue to love this cocktail bar that is slightly off-piste from the Naviglio, with its modern-industrial decor. The mixed drinks, and the excellent gins especially, together with the kitchen, which is open well into the wee hours, are its strong points. A creation of Elita, who organises many events in the city.

111 BAR TABACCHI LA DARSENA DA PEPPUCCIO

113 UGO

Via Corsico 12
Porta Genova ⑨
+39 02 3981 1557
ugobar.it

Ugo, a completely different, retro place, which resembles a Parisian salon, is just a short distance from Elita BAR. Even the cocktails, which accompany your aperitif served at the table, sometimes have a vintage look and feel. Ask barman Luca Vezzali for advice about more creative options. Small tables outside.

114 REBELOT DEL PONT DE FERR

Ripa di Porta
Ticinese 55
Navigli ⑨
+39 02 8419 4720
rebelotnavigli.com

Exposed bricks, a large bar, an impressive line-up of bottles and a crowd that is used to drinking and eating well. Take a seat at the tables and enjoy the nibbles that are prepared to order and always different. And if you want, you can even stay for dinner.

115 MORGANTE COCKTAIL & SOUL

Vicolo Privato
Lavandai 2-A
Porta Genova ⑨
+39 02 3594 0879
morgantecocktail.com

This bar takes its name from the owner, Gianfranco Morgante, the architect who transformed a former art gallery into a cocktail bar with a kitchen, in the historic Vicolo dei Lavandai. Over 150 options on the sophisticated drinks menu, which you can pair with freshly cooked food. A relaxing corner in the bustling Navigli.

5 places
WITH A VIEW
for a drink

---

116 **TERRAZZA TRIENNALE
– OSTERIA CON VISTA**
AT: LA TRIENNALE
DI MILANO
**Viale Alemagna
Emilio 6
Cairoli-Castello** ③
+39 02 3664 4340
osteriaconvista.it

The Osteria has huge windows that
overlook Sempione Park, offering
panoramic views right up to the
skyscrapers of Porta Nuova. Go up for
a sunset cocktail, but it's equally nice
at lunchtime when the sun falls through
the windows. There is a bar-bistro on
the ground floor. You can sunbathe in
the garden on sunny days.

117 **TERRAZZA 12**
AT: THE BRIAN & BARRY
BUILDING, 10TH FLOOR
**Via Durini 28
Duomo-San Babila** ②
+39 02 9285 3651
terrazza12.it

A colourful living room, with a decor
that is a nod to the fifties, on the 10th
floor of a shop. The chairs, cushions and
low tables with optical designs are very
popular with women. The space is small
so it's always better to book ahead.

118 **THE DOME ROOFTOP
& RESTAURANT**
**Via Giuseppe
Mazzini 2
Duomo-San Babila** ②
+39 02 2660 0449
odsweethotel.com

A good place for breakfast with friends,
a working lunch, cocktails or dinner, with
sharing plates. The Instagrammable terrace
on the seventh floor boasts superb views
of Piazza Duomo, the Galleria Vittorio
Emanuele and the Castello Sforzesco.
Part of the ODSweet Duomo Milano Hotel.

119 RADIO ROOFTOP MILAN

Via Marco Polo 18
North-East ⑤
+39 02 8422 0109
radiorooftop.com/
milan

An international setting, like the cocktail menu and food they serve here. Depending on the season, you eat inside or outside on the terrace. From here it seems as if you can almost touch the new skyscrapers of Porta Nuova with your hand. Deep-house music in the background.

120 TERRAZZA MARTINI

Piazza Armando
Diaz 7
Duomo-San Babila ②
+39 011 941 9831
martinierossi.it/
terrazze/milano

A historic terrace, part of the exclusive Martini brand circuit. This bar opened in 1958 and immediately became iconic, followed by branches in Paris, London, and São Paulo. You can attend events hosted by the brand and take mixology lessons. A charming place, with a 360-degree view of the city.

117 TERRAZZA 12

5
GAY-FRIENDLY PLACES
to meet

---

121 MONO BAR MILANO
Via Lecco 6 /
Via P. Castaldi
Porta Venezia ⑤
+39 339 4810 264

This was the first venue with a Berlin allure to open in Milan about ten years ago. Since then it's unwittingly become the base for the (very peaceful) gay colonisation in these streets, which were previously home to the Eritrean community. It continues to be popular. The managers make everyone feel at home.

122 LECCOMILANO
Via Lecco 5
Porta Venezia ⑤
+39 02 9163 9877
leccomilano.it

The name is deliberately tantalising (*lecco* means 'I lick' and is also the name of the bar's street) and the atmosphere in this little spot with cocktails made with spirits and organic products is irreverent and easy-going. Aperitif at 6 pm, with special items for vegetarians. Fridays and Saturdays are particularly fun.

123 TYPE
Via Pietro
Borsieri 34
Isola ⑩
+39 02 3653 4735

The name is derived from a typeface. The most popular time here is at happy hour, when they serve a healthy and vegetarian buffet, to be eaten in the small outdoor terrace or indoors. A place where people also gather for presentations and exhibitions.

124 TROPICAL ISLAND
AT: BASTIONI DI
PORTA VENEZIA
Porta Venezia ⑤
+39 02 2951 1599

A fashionable *chiringuito* on the bastions of Porta Venezia, at the entrance to the gardens, where cocktails, and their signature Moscow Mule, are paired with a few snacks at aperitivo time. The best time to come is on Wednesdays and Fridays, with gay-friendly 'Chiringay' parties and DJ sets.

125 NOLOSO
Via Luigi Varanini 5
NoLo ⑤
+39 331 4294 088

The name has a double meaning. The bar is in the neighbourhood that is now called NoLo 'North of Loreto' (New York-style) and NoLoSo literally means 'I don't know' in Italian. A colourful place, with books everywhere, even in the bathroom. During happy hour, they serve a copious vegetarian buffet. Brunch on Sundays. Fridays and Saturdays DJ sets. Tuesdays table games.

121 MONO BAR MILANO

5 places for
READING AND DRINKING COFFEE

---

126 JOY BAR
AT: BIBLIOTECA
VALVASSORI PERONI
**Via Carlo Valvassori
Peroni 56
East** ⑥
+39 349 750 8744

Situated in the Lambrate district, this is both a library cafe and a cultural project. The spaces, which were designed by the students of renowned architect Stefano Boeri, are fresh and bright, even outdoors. Read under the covered terrace or in the sun, and in the evenings there's always something on, including courses, workshops and concerts.

127 INCIPIT23
**Via Casoretto 42
North-East** ⑥
+39 378 302 9659
incipit23.cafe

A tiny publishing house that promotes independent and original voices that are just waiting to be heard. Browse the shelves for your next read and have breakfast, a light lunch or aperitivo with friends. The mixologists at the bar are happy to suggest great cocktails and reading tips!

128 RED FELTRINELLI

Corso Garibaldi 1
Brera-Corso
Garibaldi ①

The RED (RED stands for Read, Eat and Dream) LaFeltrinelli chain's fifth branch in the city. The bookshop/bar is located on two floors (350 sqm) in two renovated, early twentieth-century buildings and can seat 80. From the upper floor balcony that looks just like the *case di ringhiera* (guard rail houses), you can look right into the ground-floor bar/bistro.

129 COLIBRÌ CAFFÈ LETTERARIO

Via Laghetto 9-11
Porta Romana ②
+39 02 7639 4899
colibrimilano.it

A cosy corner behind the State University that draws a young crowd. This literary cafe has a pleasant patio in the evenings, at aperitivo time. There's a free book exchange, they often organise events and live music concerts. In Italian, *colibrì* is a little bird, but also the contraction of the words 'coffee' and 'books' (*libri* in Italian).

130 BOOKCITY

bookcitymilano.it

During the BookCity event, readings start early in the morning with a cup of coffee, and continue uninterrupted in the most diverse places throughout the city, from historic cafes to more fashionable and Instagrammable ones, but also parks (if the sun is out), libraries, museums and even private homes. There are also workshops, exhibitions, and many opportunities for meet-and-greets with authors.

5 places with a
FASHIONABLE TWIST

**131 ARMANI /
BAMBOO BAR**
Via Alessandro
Manzoni 31
Brera-Corso
Garibaldi ①
+39 02 8883 8888
*armanihotel
milano.com*

The elegant and pared down Armani /
Bamboo Bar, with its warm tones and
furniture in neutral colours, has a large
window that opens out on the city from
above. A cocoon-like environment, even
on the most chaotic days, where you can
eat a light lunch or have an aperitif. But
the bar is mostly known for its cocktails.

132 CERESIO 7
Via Ceresio 7
North-West ⑩
+39 02 3103 9221
ceresio7.com

Perhaps the most beautiful terrace in
Milan. Not because of its height, but
because a ray of sunshine is enough
to make you feel like you're on holiday
in the Dsquared2 bar by the swimming
pool. A trendy place for drinks and
dinner, which is even lovelier at
lunchtime, especially on clear days,
when you can see the mountains in
the distance.

133 BULGARI HOTEL

Via Privata Fratelli Gabba 7-B
Brera-Corso Garibaldi ①
+39 02 8058 051
bulgarihotels.com

A tranquil green oasis, created by the landscape architect Sophie Agata Ambroise, which is also open to non-hotel guests. It has a common area and some 'private rooms', among the branches of trees and shrubs and a gazebo where you can enjoy dinner. Inside the hotel you'll also find the restaurant led by chef Niko Romito (of the three Michelin-starred Reale di Castel di Sangro, in Abruzzo).

134 THE SMALL

Via Niccolò Paganini 3
North-East ⑤
+39 02 2024 0943
thesmall.it

A tiny bistro that is a veritable *Wunderkammer* and just the place to snap up some vintage and more modern furniture, including classic statues and pink flamingos, quilted velvet sofas and sixties-style chairs. The brainchild of accessory and handbag designer Giancarlo Petriglia who pays tribute to the cuisine of his native Puglia with the menu.

135 BAR MARTINI – DOLCE & GABBANA

Corso Venezia 15
Duomo-San Babila ①
+39 02 7601 1154
dolcegabbana.it

Dolce & Gabbana joined forces with Martini in a hidden location in Corso Venezia. If it weren't for the security, you wouldn't even notice the tables in the courtyard and the baroque-style interiors, which are the brand's signature. The cuisine and appetizers with your aperitif are inspired by the flavours of Sicily.

5
CO-WORKING SPACES
with a cafe

---

136 OTTO
Via Paolo Sarpi 8
Chinatown ⑩
sarpiotto.com

A space for public relations. Creatives have turned this into their office, and when you stop working – at lunchtime and around aperitivo time – it feels as if you know everyone. Have a glass of wine with some cured meats and *quadrotti*, open sandwiches with various fillings. Brunch on Sundays.

137 HUG
Via Venini 83
NoLo ⑤
+39 389 848 5296
hugmilano.com

This place in a former chocolate factory is the hot new place to go. The co-workers have their own separate space, while the cafe-bistro is open full-time, from breakfast in the morning and a snack with homemade cakes, until the evening when it's time for drinks and the lights are dimmed and candles lit.

140 **TIPOGRAFIA ALIMENTARE**

138 COFFICE

Via Olona 11
Sant'Ambrogio ④
+39 02 9157 3021
cofficemilano.it

A young and informal place, where you can work, study, meet friends and classmates. You pay for a workstation, which comes with access to coffee, tea, a buffet with sweet and savoury snacks, printers, and fast Wi-Fi. Perfect, that is if your intention wasn't to stay away from the fridge at home.

139 OPEN MILANO

Viale Monte Nero 6
Porta Romana ②
+39 02 8342 5610
openmilano.com

One of the first co-working spaces to open in Milan, Open Milano is a 1000-square-metre library with large windows, a 20-metre-long communal table, additional tables, chairs and armchairs near the bookshelves. There's also a bar and a wide range of events.

140 TIPOGRAFIA ALIMENTARE

Via Dolomiti 1
North-West ⑩
+39 02 8353 7868
tipografiaalimentare.it

Two women – a journalist and a graduate in food sciences from the University of Pollenzo, which was established by the Slow Food movement – invented this new format. Open from breakfast until aperitivo time, on the Martesana canal, this place also serves dishes made with excellent products at reasonable prices for lunch. The fast Wi-Fi for co-workers is an added bonus.

5 places for a drink with
MUSIC

---

141 BLUE NOTE MILANO
Via Pietro Borsieri 37
Isola ⑩
+39 02 6901 6888
bluenotemilano.com

The trendy and Milanese version of the Blue Note in New York. A very large, beautiful space, that is popular with jazz enthusiasts and the uninitiated alike. The artists here are largely American – all the big names drop in. There are also nights with emerging Italian artists.

142 SANTERIA SOCIAL CLUB
Viale Toscana 31
South-East ⑦
+39 02 2219 9381
santeria.milano.it

The Santeria Social Club project, which originally started at Via Paladini 8 (a bar, restaurant and co-working space that is still open), lives on in a former car dealership. Attracting young people and artists, this is a creative factory of about 1000 square metres, with a large bar and kitchen, a theatre, and, above all, many spaces for art and music.

143 SPIRIT DE MILAN

Via Bovisasca 57-59
North-West ⑩
+39 366 721 5569
spiritdemilan.it

Spirit de Milan is a restaurant with live music in a former glassworks, away from the centre. Above all, it is a fun place to enjoy 'old Milan'. You'll learn the dialect, take a few steps of swing, and sing. On Sunday evenings, the bar also hosts jazz concerts.

144 NEPENTHA CLUB

Piazza
Armando Diaz 1
Duomo-San Babila ②
+39 02 804 837
nepenthaclub.com

This dinner club has been a nightlife hotspot since 1969, attracting celebrities from the worlds of entertainment, the arts and music over the years. It is also a place that has moved with the times, which explains why it's still so wildly popular with today's in-crowd, who flock here for the DJ sets and themed nights with artists, dancers and performers. Guest list only, both for dinner and afterwards. The best evening to go? Monday according to those in the know.

145 APOLLO MILANO

Via Giosuè Borsi 9
Navigli ⑨
+39 02 3826 0176
apollomilano.com

Milan's under 30s crowd loves to hang out at the Apollo Milano, where they enjoy Mediterranean cuisine – by Apulian chef Gennaro Balice (who previously worked under Luigi Taglienti at Lume Milano) –, classic and innovative cocktails by Simone Sanna and great music. Friday is the best night to go, going by the Instagram posts of Milan's music scene. *Bella lì* (as the Milanese tend to say

RINASCENTE

40 PLACES
TO SHOP

---

5 wonderful places to smell
F L O W E R S

146 FIORAIO BIANCHI CAFFÈ

Via Montebello 7
Brera-Corso
Garibaldi ①
+39 02 2901 4390
fioraiobianchicaffe.it

Milan's first flower shop with a bistro charm has managed to retain much of its charm. At the entrance you'll find a wooden counter and many tables where you can have a coffee at breakfast time, enjoy a light lunch at midday or meet for drinks later in the day. Perfect for an intimate chat, with elegant floral arrangements and the discreet scent of flowers wafting around you.

147 POTAFIORI

Via Salasco 17
South-East ⑦
+39 02 8706 5930
potafiori.com
fiorirosalba.it

The owner, Rosalba Piccinni, says she is a singer-florist. To enjoy one of her greatest passions, she decided to open a flower shop years ago (Via Giuseppe Broggi 17). More recently, she has also added a space where you can have drinks or dine among the flowers and plants. The atmosphere heats up when she starts to sing.

148 FIORAIO BOLLETTINI
Via Massimo Gorki 2
South-West ⑨
+39 02 4233 020

It looks like a garden, albeit enclosed by walls whose colours blend in with those of the flowers and artful compositions, in an absolutely natural and equally magical way. Choose the most suitable flowers for the occasion, with some help from the owner or just treat yourself to something special of your own choice.

149 W FIORI – WALTER VALENTE
Via Melzo 2
Porta Venezia ⑤
+39 02 3653 0346
wfiori.it

If you love orchids, this is the place for you. Walter Valente's shop showcases sophisticated combinations, in a tiny shop window full of details, vases and special containers. Much loved by women's magazine editors and the fashion world that relies on him for events.

150 FLOWER MARKET IN NAVIGLI
Along Naviglio Grande
Navigli ⑨
+39 02 8940 9971
navigliogrande.mi.it

Perhaps you may have noticed that houses in Milan have terraces that are overflowing with beautiful flowers. Gardening borders on the obsessive here, and even balconies and walkways are planted. In April and October, more than 200 nurseries from all over Italy exhibit their products at the Fiori e Sapori market on the Naviglio. A great opportunity for some green shopping, even if the effect is in technicolour.

5 *old-school*
STATIONERY SHOPS

151 RIGADRITTO

Via Brera 6
Brera-Corso
Garibaldi ①
+39 02 8058 2936

The first stop for stationery, where paper and 'derivatives' are combined with objects that the owner, Roberta Naj Oleari, finds all over the world. From pencil cases to notepads, and fun, eclectic and whacky pop-up cards. So much for toeing the line: here they believe in colouring outside the lines.

152 ANTICA CARTOLERIA NOVECENTO DAL 1899

Piazza Risorgimento 3
East ⑥
+39 02 7600 6123

Located in a historic building, this is one of the many historic shops in Milan. This beautiful stationery shop was established at the end of the 1800s and has been in the caring hands of several families of stationers. The shop has retained the original furnishings. The iron windows and dark wood furniture give it a very special allure.

153 PASINI 1922

Viale Tibaldi 3
South-West ⑨
+39 02 5810 0876
pasinicarta.it

Here materials to bind books, volumes and encyclopaedias take centre stage. A popular place for people who want to put together their own family recipe book, a photo album or a scrapbook and paradise on earth for fans of cartonnage and découpage.

154 PISOTTI

Alzaia Naviglio
Grande 98
Navigli ⑨
+39 02 8940 3348
pisotti.it

Do you like precious paper, antique and classic graphic designs with the Florentine lily? Or more contemporary motifs in a wide variety of colours and sizes? A place that is particular popular with calligraphy lovers or creative souls who like to make special cards or origami.

155 FRATELLI BONVINI

Via Tagliamento 1
South-East ⑦
+39 02 5392 151
bonvini1909.com

In the early 1900s, this was a stationery shop and a printer's. It was saved from closure and restored to its former glory. Today its drawers and shelves are full of pencils, pens, ink and stamps. Bonvini organises courses, events about typography, art publishing, writing and drawing in its Atelier 1909, just around the corner on Corso Lodi.

5 not-to-miss
BOOKSHOPS

156 STAMBERGA

Via Melzo 3
Porta Venezia ⑤
+39 335 563 6433
stamberga.it

Hidden in the inner courtyard of an art nouveau building in a highly creative area, this art space with exposed brick walls and a concrete floor houses books, objects, artworks, jewellery and photographs: 'Spiritus' is the permanent exhibition of photographer Marco Beretta's work. In Italian, the word *stamberga* is used to describe an inhospitable environment, but here it is obviously used ironically, because it is indeed a very pleasant place to meet and gather.

157 MAMU MAGAZZINO MUSICA

Via Soave 3
South-East ⑦
+39 02 3668 6303
magazzinomusica.it

You'll find both new and used sheet music, books – even non-fiction and fiction with a music focus – and CDs here. And last but not least, a wide variety of musical instruments. MaMu is also a space for cultural events, master classes, and book presentations, and where there is always time to talk about classical music.

158 LIBRERIA DELLO SPETTACOLO

Via Terraggio 11
Sant'Ambrogio ④
+39 02 8645 1730
*libreriadello
spettacolo.it*

Posters and photographs, books about cinema, theatre, circus and dance; volumes that describe the evolution of radio and television. A Wunderkammer where one never gets tired of leafing through scripts, screenplays and specialist periodicals and listening to the stories of the owner, Maria Cristina Spigaglia.

159 121+

Via Savona 17/5
Porta Genova ⑨
+39 02 3658 4119
corraini.com

A large bright space in a brick house where you will find a hand-picked selection of books on architecture, art, graphics and photography. 121+ is owned by the historic Corraini publishing house, which specialises in illustration and design, of which it has a complete catalogue. They also sell a nice selection of children's books, including by Bruno Munari.

160 FONDAZIONE FELTRINELLI

Viale Pasubio 5
North-West ⑩
+39 02 4958 341
fondazionefeltrinelli.it

It's been compared to a Gothic church with large windows. The new Feltrinelli headquarters, built on land that belonged to the family since the 1800s and designed by the Herzog & de Meuron studio, have been perfectly integrated in the urban setting. An archive, a book shop, bar and Microsoft's headquarters, this building won the award for best urban renewal project at MIPIM 2018.

The 5 best places for
BICYCLE ADDICTS

---

161 BICI&RADICI

Via Nicola d'Apulia 2
NoLo ⑤
+39 02 8341 8589
bicieradici.com

A delightful place in Piazza Morpegno, where the tram rattles by and where Stefania and Marco open a place that caters to plant and bicycle lovers. The owners are happy to share tips and tricks as well as manuals to green your life. You can also rent a bike and head to Parco Trotter or Parco della Martesana.

162 UPCYCLE MILANO BIKE CAFÉ

Via Ampère 59
East ⑥
+39 02 8342 8268
upcyclecafe.it

Italy's first self-proclaimed 'Cafe Bistrot'. We don't know whether this is true. You can spend an afternoon studying or working here, and in the evening, you can often enjoy live music. Don't worry about the huge portion sizes, you can burn off the calories by biking home.

163 ROSSIGNOLI

163 ROSSIGNOLI

Corso Garibaldi 65-71
Brera-Corso
Garibaldi ①
+39 02 804 960
rossignoli.it

They have been making their own
bicycles here for over 100 years, fixing
them in the workshop, and selling them,
along with those of famous brands. There
is a sense of history in this shop, where
the same family has worked for five
generations, assisted by their competent
staff. Like Piero, who won the Corriere
della Sera title of 'Best salesman in Milan'.

164 LA STAZIONE DELLE BICICLETTE-URBAN STYLE

Corso Lodi 66
South-East ⑦
+39 02 5560 3730
lastazione
dellebiciclette.com

Another address for riders in search of
a custom bicycle, made entirely by hand,
that reflects the tastes and needs of its
rider. Just tell the young owners what you
have in mind. It will be perfect for the
city or, depending on your requirements,
for a ride to the seaside or the mountains.

165 LA CICLISTICA MILANO

Via Pellizza da
Volpedo 12
West ⑧
+39 02 3655 0328
laciclisticamilano.it

Two friends came up with the idea of
this project when it became fashionable
again to ride a bike: bike lanes were
opened and bikes and co-ops were in
high demand. They have a handmade
collection of made in Italy models. The
bikes are beautiful, solid and affordable,
and come with an unlimited warranty.

The 5 loveliest
TEXTILE SHOPS

166 **BONATI & BONEGGI**
Via Enrico Toti 4
Sant'Ambrogio ④
+39 02 8646 4537
bonatiebeneggi.it

For over 80 years, the Milanese have turned to this family business for their fabrics and furniture. Founder Alberto Riva imported only the best American and British brands. Today Bonati & Beneggi offers a well-curated selection of upholstery fabrics and wallpaper. Its exquisite showroom is a great place to find inspiration to revamp your home.

167 **SILVA**
Via Olona 25
Sant'Ambrogio ④
+39 02 8940 0788
silvatessuti.it

Right now palm trees are all the range, before this everyone was entranced by optical patterns. Who knows what the future will bring? The graphic designs for curtains, cushions and sofas anticipate and follow trends. They mainly sell Italian and European products here as well as a few American brands and wallpaper, too.

168 TESSUTI E SCAMPOLI

Via Lario 14
Isola ⑩
+39 02 6886 493
tessutiescampoli.it

You are advised to come early. This two-storey shop offers a huge selection of fabrics, scraps, haberdashery – buttons, zippers, sequins, feathers of all types and colours – and is a treasure trove for design students, who also hang out there just to see what's new. If you want to be served, you'll have to have some patience.

169 LISA CORTI TESSUTI

Via Lecco 2
Porta Venezia ⑤
+39 02 2024 1483
lisacorti.com

Bold colours everywhere you look. From fabrics by the metre to cushions, curtains and sofa covers for your living room as well as everything you need to elevate your kitchen or dining room or add character to your bedroom (or that of your kids). The shop sells a nice selection of dresses, caftans, kurtas and wraps in vibrant colours.

170 NEW TESS

Via Montevideo 9
Porta Genova ⑨
+39 02 6949 0311
newtess.it

Looking around you'll notice young stylists from fashion schools, dress-makers and women sorting through a wide range of fabrics for a section of fabric for a custom-made dress. This is the outlet of the luxury brand Como Clerici Tessuto, which is world-renowned for its fine fabrics. Check the website for its opening hours.

5 tempting shops for
ONE-OF-A-KIND
OBJECTS

───────────

171 MV% CERAMICS DESIGN
Alzaia Naviglio
Grande 156
Navigli ⑨
+39 02 4771 0256
mv-ceramicsdesign.it

Clouds, drops, stars and flowers. As well as cups, plates and letters; all in ceramic, all handmade, for you to hang in the kitchen, the living room or your children's room. Welcome to the world of Mariavera Chiari, who makes all the objects on sale in this shop on the Naviglio, with its beautiful wisteria at the entrance. Also has an online shop.

172 FORNASETTI
Corso Venezia 21-A
Porta Venezia ①
+39 02 8416 1374
fornasetti.com

Eclectic and optimistic: this perfectly sums up the spirit of founder Piero Fornasetti, whose ceramics with female faces smile mysteriously from the shop window. Walking through the various rooms, you can revisit the brand's history. If you love opera, then buy the Don Giovanni CD, in Fornasetti's version, of course.

173 FORNACE CURTI

Via Walter Tobagi 8
South-West ⑨
+39 02 8135 049
fornacecurti.it

A place of rare charm, a tiny village with ancient houses and plants, workshops and ovens, and 20 studios of artists, painters and photographers. With a history that commenced in the 1400s, the period in which these terracotta craftsmen started producing pottery with deep red clay from the Po Valley. Open the third weekend of May or by appointment.

174 ALGRANTI LAB

Via Guglielmo
Pepe 20-28
Isola ⑩
+39 349 318 8432
algrantilab.it

They give reclaimed materials a new lease on life, building new furniture and highlighting the history of wood, iron, aluminium, terracotta and copper. The latter is taken from roofs, from gutters, flashings, and converses. Directed by Pietro Algranti, the lab was founded by Costanza Algranti in 1997. Opening hours: 10 am – 1 pm and 3 pm – 7 pm, Saturdays by appointment.

175 LABORATORIO PARAVICINI

Via Nerino 8
5vie ②
+39 02 7202 1006
paravicini.it

In a hidden courtyard in the historic centre lies this 20-year-old Wunder-kammer where hand-painted and printed objects like dishes and tableware are created. The designs are classically inspired, with dreamy and exotic elements like snakes, jugglers, and hot air balloons, and can be made to measure. Benedetta and Margherita, Costanza Paravicini's daughters, are the workshop's most creative and modern designers.

5 shops to
FEEL BEAUTIFUL

176 MADAME MIRANDA
madamemiranda.com

An on-demand service that can be booked at all times of the day (6 am - 11 pm). Need a mani that's fast as lightning, a blowout before a business meeting or a relaxing massage after a long day of shopping? A professional will come to your house with everything you need. Even for a beauty party!

177 BAHAMA MAMA
Viale Col di Lana 1
South-East ⑦
+39 02 8940 4538
bahamamama.it

A nail bar and a place to relax. The name refers to a nail polish and a cocktail. Bahama Mama has a cosy interior, with neutral colours. The staff here only use natural products, for manicure and pedicure treatments. If you are in the mood for some shopping, they also have a clothes corner.

178 BELLAVERA

Piazza Buonarroti 32
West ⑧
+30 02 4398 6566
bellavera.it

Imagine a beautician who tells you the truth, in a very direct way. She's a cynical beautician, the most beloved blogger in Milan *(estetistacinica.it)*, a true star in the world of online beauty. BellaVera is her wellness centre, where you can book specific treatments. Go and do not try to soften her because we like her just the way she is.

179 MY PLACE HAIR STUDIO

Via Panizza 4
West ⑧
+39 02 3675 3350
myplacehairstudio.com

They mainly use natural and organic products, henna hair dye combined with organic pigments, and restructuring oils for healthy hair and skin. The salon of hair stylist Tommaso Incamicia feels a bit like at home, because of the intimate atmosphere and the fact there is always a herbal tea waiting for you.

180 KULT MILANO

Corso San Gottardo 3
South-West ⑨
+39 02 3656 5508
kultmilano.com

This place moved to a hidden place, a courtyard in the old Milan area, but essentially it has remained the same. Check out this vintage style hairdresser's – they are famous for their 'crazy' hair dyes – and tattoo studio. Every month they host different artists to develop new ideas and offer a wider range of styles.

The 5 most high-end
DEPARTMENT STORES

181 BRIAN AND BARRY

Via Durini 28
Duomo-San Babila ②
+39 02 9285 3547
brianebarry.it

Brian and Barry calls itself a 'boutique department store' and is housed in a 1950s building designed by the architect Giovanni Muzio. This shop, which is centrally located, has twelve floors dedicated to shopping and an intriguing corner dedicated to watchmaking. The sartorial element, for which the store is well-known, is also inherent in the cuisine of its rooftop restaurant Asola, where chef Matteo Torretta wields the sceptre.

182 RINASCENTE

Piazza Duomo
Duomo-San Babila ②
+39 02 9138 7388
rinascente.it

The poet Gabriele d'Annunzio came up with this department store's name in 1917. The advertising was entrusted to Marcello Dudovich and Giò Ponti was asked to create a collection of modern furnishings. Easy to see how this department store became so popular with the bourgeoisie, because of the tasteful objects it sold and the opportunity for renewal it created. Rinascente has reached the 21st century unscathed, and stronger than ever.

183 COIN

Piazza Cinque
Giornate 1-A
East ⑥
+39 02 5519 2083
coin.it

Another story of entrepreneurship, which started in 1916 with a 'street vendor's license' in the province of Venice and which went on to become one of the biggest Italian department stores in the post-war period. They have had a branch in Milan since the 1960s, with ten floors in glass and metal. This 'showcase' continues to sell 'Made in Italy' and collections by young creative designers.

184 HIGHTECH

Via Venticinque
Aprile 12
North-West ⑩
+39 02 624 1101
cargomilano.it

The Milanese adore this shop off elegant Corso Como. An intricate maze where you can find anything from home décor items and fabrics and light fixtures to small items of furniture and utensils for the kitchen as well as a selection of clothes. Try not to get lost as you make your way through the rooms and up the stairs.

185 CITYLIFE SHOPPING DISTRICT

Piazza Tre Torri 1L
West ⑧
+39 02 4349 5911
citylife
shoppingdistrict.it

The latest addition to the city, near the CityLife skyscrapers, was designed by Zaha Hadid. Inside, you can see how skilfully she selected and used materials, such as bamboo, for one of the largest and most up-to-date urban shopping districts in Europe, with one hundred shops on three floors. Aimed at an upper-middle class clientele.

ROSSANA ORLANDI

55 PLACES
FOR FASHION
& DESIGN

---

5 creative places to shop
VINTAGE CLOTHES

---

186 CAVALLI E NASTRI
Via Brera 2
Brera-Corso
Garibaldi ①
+39 02 7200 0449
cavallienastri.com

Stylists know they can always find the finishing flourish for that outfit for a photo shoot. One of the city's first vintage shops, it combines collectors' items – from Chanel jewellery to original 1950s Borsalino hats – with small furnishings. It also has other locations.

187 MADAME PAULINE
Foro Buonaparte 74
Cairoli-Castello ③
+39 02 4943 1201
madamepauline
vintage.it

This small shop in the Castello area is a treasure trove of wonders, where you can lose yourself admiring designer items – wonderful accessories and clothes by Hermès, Chanel, Prada – or chatting with the owner who showcases them with extreme care. Because sometimes a glamourous detail is enough to make an outfit unforgettable.

188 VINTAGE DELIRIUM
Via Giuseppe
Sacchi 3
Brera-Corso
Garibaldi ①
+39 02 8646 2076
vintagedelirium.it

Franco Jacassi combines his experience working in the art world, being a keen collector and his passion for fashion in this shop. He sells garments by Vionnet, Schiaparelli, Pucci and YSL as well as antique fabrics, laces and buttons, of which Jacassi has a magnificent collection.

189 HUMANA

Via Cappellari 3
Duomo-San Babila ②
+39 02 7208 0606
humanavintage.it

Trendier than the other locations around Europe. After all, this is Milan. The favourite hunting ground of fashion editors, who find original items and accessories from the sixties and seventies here, which are perfect for completing a look. Proceeds go towards development projects in the South.

190 EAST MARKET

Via Mecenate 88
South-East ⑦
+39 392 043 0853
eastmarketmilano.com

A London-style market with a Milanese twist in an industrial space, which sells vintage and handmade clothes and accessories. There is no shortage of modern antiques, music and books here. And food naturally, with lots of food trucks. No set calendar: alerts are sent by e-mail. Alternatively you can check online.

190 EAST MARKET

5 places to discover
NEW DESIGNERS

191 BIFFI BOUTIQUES

Corso Genova 6
Sant'Ambrogio ④
+39 02 8311 6052
biffi.com

People who work in the fashion industry know Rosy Biffi, an internationally-renowned trendsetter. Since the 1960s, this taste-maker has identified trends and designers with the same infallible instinct, suggesting Mary Quant's mini-skirts and Stella McCartney's creations to her loyal clientele over the years.

192 WAIT AND SEE

Via Santa Marta 14
5vie ②
+39 02 7208 0195
waitandsee.it

You'll need to search for this shop, which is hidden in the streets of old Milan. But how can you resist the explosion of colour and creativity that awaits you. Enter the former 18th-century convent and browse this welcoming multi-brand store. Many styles of clothing, accessories, jewellery, including some vintage items.

193 ANTONIA MILANO
AT: PALAZZO CAGNOLA
Via Cusani 5
Brera-Corso
Garibaldi ①
+39 02 8699 8340
antonia.it

Antonia Giacinti's name has become synonymous with a fine selection of contemporary and experimental fashion brands. Her shop is located in Palazzo Cagnola, a 19th-century building that was renovated by the architect Vincenzo de Cotiis. Explore over 600 square metres with marble furnishings, soft fabrics and plexiglass fixtures, to find the most sought-after apparel. Also for men.

194 SLAM JAM
Via Giovanni Lanza 1
Cairoli-Castello ③
+39 02 8909 3965
slamjam.com

The place to be for streetwear fans. The Ferrara company opened this shop, combining comfortable 'street-style' clothes with music, visual arts and lifestyle, offering customers an all-in experience. Brands include Undercover, Fear of God, Visvim and limited-edition sneakers.

195 WOK STORE
Col di Lana 5-A
South-East ⑦
+39 02 3656 8742
wok-store.com

Cosmopolitan Wok sells many different brands, including some unusual items from around the world. It tries hard – and succeeds – to be original and eccentric. Interesting men's and entertainment section, which often also includes DJ sets in the store. Definitely not for everyone, and this also applies to the prices. Available online.

5 stylish shops for
WOMEN

196 TANTRIKA SHOP

Via Antonio
Pollaiuolo 2
Isola ⑩
+39 699 003 22

Tantrika is all about Cristina, who transformed a small workshop in the Isola district into her kingdom, which is renowned for its clothes and colours, which are all natural and all very carefully selected. She also sells some jewellery. Prices are never excessive, which is a nice bonus.

197 MEMÈM VIA SAVONA

197 MEMÈM VIA SAVONA

Via Savona 1
Porta Genova ⑨
+39 02 3675 3846

To find out what's available at Memèm's, even before making the trek to this outpost of Tortona, check their Instagram profile at *@mememviasavona*. A virtual shop window for the young owner's picks, all with a French allure (and sometimes also from France).

198 LAURA URBINATI

Viale Col di Lana 8,
2° cortile
South-East ⑦
+39 02 8372 573
lauraurbinati.com

Laura's swimwear, which has the advantage of looking good even on ordinary mortals, is famous. It works fine on every body type, thanks to the stylist's expert advice. Laura Urbinati hails from Rome, her designs are very simple and everything is made in Italy.

199 RAPA STORE

Via Pastrengo 5-A
Isola ⑩
+39 02 2316 7868
rapa-store.com

A soft, cosy, colourful style, that's quintessentially Italian. Created by Paola and Sara for their small boutique in the Isola district. Take a peek at the window, be tempted, step inside and then pick up some of their casual-chic clothes, in many different colours. Practical and beautiful, very suitable and fun to wear, also for children.

200 MARIZA TASSY

Via Molino delle
Armi 45
Ticinese ②
+39 02 8941 5364
marizatassy.it

Lella and Paola Rigante, the owners who have excellent taste, named the shop after their Franco-Turkish grandmother who designed clothes for the upper-crust ladies of Istanbul in the early 20th century. This tiny multi-brand store sells items by talented designers, from around the world. The apple doesn't fall far from the tree.

5 cool shops for
MEN'S CLOTHES

---

201 CIVICONOVE

Via Bartolomeo
Eustachi 33
Porta Venezia ⑤
+39 02 8407 0913

Paolo Simonetta and Luca Lazzaro, both passionate about everything contemporary, started this space dedicated to fashion and art. It is now one of the most interesting spots for those searching for new brands and designers, which the owners scout around the world. Not just clothes – and not only for men – but also accessories, bags, shoes, and perfumes are on offer in this minimal space, where nothing is left to chance.

202 CALZE GALLO

Via Manzoni 16
Duomo-San Babila ①
+39 02 783 602
gallo1927.com

These colourful socks – with stripes, diamonds and polka dots – look equally nice in an important meeting. Why not show them off when you cross your legs, as they peek out from between your trousers and your dress shoes. But they are also a must-have for the weekend, when the patterns can be even more fun and playful. Always made from high-quality yarns.

203 GENIALI MILANO

Via Vincenzo Monti /
Via Aurelio Saffi 7
Cairoli-Castello ③
+39 02 462 606
genialimilano.com

A multi-brand store for men's fashion, selling some of the most high-end Made in Italy lines – Ernesto, Lardini, Settefili Cashmere – combining a classic and sporty style with a tailor-made service. Suits for the office and warm jumpers for the weekend, as well as colourful scarves and refined accessories. And some very nice shoes.

204 BOGLIOLI

Via San Pietro
all'Orto 17
Duomo-San Babila ②
+39 02 7639 4051
boglioli.it

This sophisticated shop, which is located in one of the most chic areas of Milan, sells the elegant textiles of the eponymous Italian brand. Originally a tailor's, Boglioli soon became an established name, using fine fabrics for some classic tailoring.

205 MUTINELLI CAPPELLI

Corso Buenos Aires 5
Porta Venezia ⑤
+39 02 2952 3594
*mutinellicappelli
milano.com*

The sign reads 'founded in 1888'. Inside, you can still see the original floors, the wood panelling and the wrought iron. They sell walking sticks and suspenders, but hats are the real star of the show, in an endless range of shapes and sizes, with several old Italian brands.

The 5 best shops for surprising
ACCESSORIES

---

206 PORSELLI

Piazza P. Ferrari 6
Duomo-San Babila ②
+39 02 8053 759
porselli.it

Milanese women love them, although their partners don't. These ballet flats, which were originally created for ballerinas, soon became one of the most popular shoes on the street. This Milanese brand, which was founded by Eugenio Porselli in 1919, continues to produce them and is still a great hit with women. New arrivals in the shop on Wednesdays.

207 LE SOLFERINE

Via Solferino 2
Brera-Corso
Garibaldi ①
+39 02 6555 352
lesolferine.com

Another classic Milanese icon, which was founded in the late nineties. The brand works with Italian artisans to produce original shoes with a simple design, using high-quality leather made in Italy. They also own Le Vintage store, in Via Garigliano 4, in the Isola neighbourhood.

208 LES AMIS CALZATURE

Corso Garibaldi 127
Brera-Corso
Garibaldi ①
+39 02 653 061
lesa2miscalzature.wixsite.com/lesamiscalzature

A tiny shop for shoe addicts. The shop window displays the handmade shoes, all made in Italy: from very elegant sandals to stiletto pumps, biker boots and knee boots. You'll find all the latest fashion trends – just make sure you have your credit card with you.

209 SEX SADE

Via Felice Casati 8
Porta Venezia ⑤
+39 02 2953 7299
sex-sade.it

Catering solely to women, to please and pleasure, while playing a game of seduction, albeit always with a hint of irony. From lingerie and beautiful corsets to retro-style dresses – but you can also find a hot nurse outfit here – to latex and PVC clothing, including footwear. Nothing vulgar, even in the sex toy section.

210 MERCATO SETTIMANALE

Via Giovanni
Batista Fauchè
West ⑧

Via San Marco
Brera-Corso
Garibaldi ①
mercati-settimanali.it

Two open-air markets, which are very popular with Milanese ladies. Here you'll find a stand that sells Forte dei Marmi cashmere, and another selling designer shoes. Hopefully they stock your size. Via Fauchè: Tuesdays 7.30 am – 2 pm, Saturdays until 6 pm. San Marco: Mondays and Thursdays 7.30 am – 2 pm.

206 PORSELLI

5 original
CONCEPT STORES

211 MODES
Piazza Risorgimento 8
East ⑥
+39 02 4549 7839
modes.com

This 400-square-metre space designed by architect Andrea Caputo, with a very flexible layout, is a place of research. They offer everything from clothing to jewellery, perfumes, and flowers. It also serves as a place for cultural reflection, with their 'literary lounge'.

212 NONOSTANTE MARRAS
Via Cola di Rienzo 8
South-West ⑨
+39 02 8907 5002
antoniomarras.com

This concept store is located in a former workshop, which is tucked away in a flowery courtyard. A dreamlike space, which is also an art gallery, a meeting venue with antique sofas and furniture and large chandeliers. In the centre, you can find clothes made from special fabrics, surrounded by flowers, books and artworks.

213 SIX GALLERY
Via Scaldasole 7
Sant'Ambrogio ④
+39 02 4548 9540
six-gallery.com

A hidden space in a courtyard with a landscape architecture studio and a design studio with eclectic furniture from the early 20th century to the 1970s. The bistro, the Sixième, has a few tables and a large cocktail bar. The new Sister hotel was designed by entrepreneur Mauro Orlandelli, founder of the Six Project.

214 GARAGE ITALIA

Viale Certosa 86 /
Piazzale Accursio 1
North-West ⑩
+39 02 3343 1857
+39 02 2222 0307
(restaurant)
garage-italia.com

Opened by Lapo Elkann, the scion of the Agnelli dynasty, Garage Italia customises all means of transportation, from scooters to off-road vehicles, and even helicopters! It's located in the former Agip Supercortemaggiore gas station, known as the 'spaceship', which was commissioned by ENI's founder Enrico Mattei. The building, which has been restored, has a cocktail bar and a restaurant.

215 ROSSANA ORLANDI

Via Matteo
Bandello 14-16
Sant'Ambrogio ④
+39 02 4674 471
rossanaorlandi.com

Rossana Orlandi has established her creative space in a former tie factory. The original setting, wall furniture and stairs surround an infinite number of drawers. Don't forget to check out the bistRo: she joined forces with one of Milan's most popular restaurants, Il luogo di Aimo and Nadia *(aimoenadia.com)*, for this project.

213 SIX GALLERY

5 must-visit
DESIGN GALLERIES

216 GALLERIA LUISA DELLE PIANE

Via Giusti 24
Chinatown ⑩
+39 02 3319 680
*gallerialuisa
dellepiane.it*

The elegant Milanese gallery owner Luisa Delle Piane is well-known in the industry. Her research into the decorative arts of the 20th century began in the 1970s, and continues unabated today. An ever-attentive interpreter of cultural change, she organises interesting exhibitions and installations and creates some exclusive pieces of furniture.

217 GALLERIA CLIO CALVI RUDY VOLPI

Via Pontaccio 17
Brera-Corso
Garibaldi ①
+39 02 8691 5009
cliocalvirudyvolpi.it

An address to add to your travel notebook. The Clio Calvi and Rudy Volpi gallery shows the work of such artists as Andrea Branzi, Haruka Fujita, Harush Shlomo and Nicoletta Morozzi, always offering a refined and never boring perspective on art. Its exhibitions are among the most popular in Milan.

218 GALLERIA ANNA MARIA CONSADORI

Via Brera 2
Brera-Corso
Garibaldi ①
+39 02 7202 1767
galleriaconsadori.com

Ceramics, lamps, and furnishings created by designers such as Giò Ponti, Ignazio Gardella and Enzo Mari are flanked by contemporary paintings and sculptures, selected by Anna Maria Consadori. The architect and daughter of the painter Silvio Consadori, her space is located in Brera, historically the artists' district.

219 RAW

Via Palermo 1
Brera-Corso
Garibaldi ①
+39 02 8494 7990
rawmilano.it

A Wunderkammer, a place where – thanks to the many decades of experience and passion of Paolo Badesco – objects of different origins and periods are shown together. The studio advises customers how to add a sophisticated and poetic touch to their homes. Head to the Corso Magenta (10) branch, which has a bar, for more vintage items.

220 DILMOS

Piazza San Marco 1
Brera-Corso
Garibaldi ①
+39 02 2900 2437
dilmos.it

The most iconic objects and pieces of contemporary furniture are displayed in a space that dates from the 1980s. They have all been chosen for their communicative value, as well as their functionality, speaking multiple languages, understanding each other, and the public. The windows of this striking space overlook Via Solferino.

The 5 best shops for
DESIGNER ITEMS

---

221 MORONI GOMMA

Corso Garibaldi 2
Brera-Corso
Garibaldi ①
+39 02 796 220
moronigomma.it

This place is one of those 'historical shops' in Milan, but it doesn't look its age at all. That's because the objects that are exhibited here are always original, featuring the latest design trends for your home, garden or studio. They also sell some small interesting gift items, as well as linear furniture upstairs.

222 KITCHEN MILANO

Via Edmondo de
Amicis 45
Sant'Ambrogio ④
+39 02 5810 2849
kitchenmilano.it

Objects, ingredients, books: the key ingredients of Kitchen, which sells kitchenware with an innovative design and inspiring cookbooks. The store also offers cooking and cocktail classes, which are very trendy at the moment.

223 FUNKY TABLE

Via Santa Marta 19
5vie ②
+39 02 3674 8619
funkytable.it

One of the most entertaining window displays in the city, which is always full of objects, that are placed on a large table or spread around the shop. Enter and look carefully as there seems to be no end to the glorious array of items to choose from! The young brand 'welcomes and selects thoughts, traditions, craftsmanship' from Italy and other countries. Always with a fun and playful twist.

224 MAGAZZINO76

Viale Padova 76
NoLo ⑤
+39 349 700 9798
magazzino76.it

Antiques and modern objects come to life at SpazioStudio78, the carpenter's workshop in this warehouse. They are then ready to be put on display and purchased by enthusiasts who will find Italian and international designer furniture from the early 20th century until the 1980s here. Everything is unique and carefully restored.

225 100FA

Viale Col di Lana 8
South-East ⑦
+39 02 8426 9136
100fa.it

A word of wisdom: do not fall in love with the vintage objects at 100FA, as you can only rent, not buy them. This space, which is not far from the Darsena and where everything is magic, has an interesting selection of industrial-style pieces of furniture (for sale), both for the home and the garden. They ship all over the world upon request.

5 amazing
JEWELLERY SHOPS

226 ARCOPARCO

Via Bertani 8
Cairoli-Castello ③
+39 329 719 0635
arcoparco.com

Lucia Giorgetti is the heart and soul behind this mini-workshop that overlooks Arco della Pace. She decorates her jewellery with her unparalleled graphics, many of which are inspired by Japanese designs. The large bracelets and earrings are unusual, and very light, because they're made of wood. She also uses glass components that are produced in Murano.

227 MONICA CASTIGLIONI

Via Pastrengo 4
Isola ⑩
+39 02 8723 7979
monicacastiglioni.com

An artist, sculptor, and photographer. Castiglioni has a workshop in Brooklyn NY, a shop in Sicily and another one in the Isola district in Milan, her hometown. Here she exhibits some unique pieces, usually jewellery cast in bronze for the most part, because she loves the solidity and the colour of this metal. Just like she loves the shape of the pistil, one of her favourite motifs.

228 PELLINI GIOIELLI

228 PELLINI GIOIELLI

Via Morigi 9
5vie ②
+39 02 7201 0213
pellini.it

Emma Caimi Pellini has had a workshop in Milan since 1947. Her daughter Carla and her niece Donatella continued the tradition, reinterpreting the art of goldsmithing. Since the eighties, they have been creating collections in plexiglass, PVC, rhodoid, and resin, a modern material that is worked in the traditional way. Three stores in Milan (one in the nearby Corso Magenta) and one in Paris.

229 DANIELA DE MARCHI

Via dei Piatti 9
5vie ②
+39 02 8699 5040
danielademarchi.it

The designer and Milanese goldsmith Daniela de Marchi creates bronze, brass and silver jewellery with natural gemstones. She has a very distinct taste, and also uses her own technique, called *dropage*, with small spheres covering the jewellery. In addition to the workshop in the Duomo area, she has a shop in Piazzale Lavater 2.

230 PETRA GIOIELLI

Via Spallanzani 11
Porta Venezia ⑤
+39 02 2953 3632
petragioielli.it

A goldsmith's shop where everything is made by hand, and every creation is absolutely unique. Jewellery with a fresh and casual design, with colour, cut, classic and unusual stones, 9-karat and 18-karat gold making it even more special. The neo-antique line is exquisite.

5 shops for unique
ANTIQUE FINDS

---

231 PENNISI JEWELLERY

Via Manzoni 29
Brera-Corso
Garibaldi ①
+39 02 862 232
gioielleriapennisi.it

Pennisi Jewellery has a long family history, with the third generation in charge of the shop. They are experts in antique jewellery and precious stones, as well as silver and *objets de vertu* such as boxes and snuffboxes, which became popular in the post-war years, in Milan. They also are passionate collectors of Chinese and Japanese art and art deco jewellery.

232 OFFICINA ANTIQUARIA

Via Pietro
Maroncelli 2
North-West ⑩
+39 02 6900 0821
officinaantiquaria.com

You can find antiques, art deco pieces, and 20th-century design in this space which is just a short distance from Corso Como. The owner, Luca Vitali, is passionate about history, art and furniture. The gallery also has a restoration workshop.

233 RICORDI E BALOCCHI

Via Donizetti 2
Porta Romana ②
+39 02 5511 786
ricordiebalocchi.com

'Doll Hospital': how can you resist stopping here when you see a sign like this? The shop has only one window, which is crowded with similar objects and which points to the selection of toys and dolls collected inside, owned by a couple of passionate collectors. The shop/workshop is very fast when it comes to repairing and restoring antique toys.

234 MERCATONE DELL'ANTIQUARIATO

Naviglio Grande
Navigli ⑨
*navigliogrande.mi.it/
mercatone-
dellantiquariato*

Walk through over 380 exhibitors of antique furniture, paintings, objects, vintage jewellery, modern and designer items, old games, records and books. All arranged on the stalls that line the banks of the Naviglio Grande, from Viale Gorizia to Via Valenza. Every last Sunday of the month.

235 AMART. ANTIQUARI MILANESI

AT: PALAZZO DELLA
PERMANENTE
Via Filippo Turati 34
Porta Nuova ①
+39 02 7750 447
amart-milano.com

This event, which is promoted by the Milanese Antiquarian Association, is organised in the neoclassical Palazzo della Permanente, which is an important venue for trade shows. Over the years, it has become a point of reference for the national and international antique market, as well as providing a platform for a cultural dialogue with the main stakeholders in this industry.

Our 5 favourite
SPECIALITY SHOPS

236 ALTALEN HATS

Via Benvenuto
Cellini 21
East ⑥
+39 02 8703 4435
altalen.it

Eclectic, playful, unique. These are the hats that are created in the workshop of Antonina 'Nafi' De Luca and Elena Todros. They work like tailors, using quality fabrics – in some cases very old ones too – transforming them into cloches, bowlers, and cylinders. The hats hang or stand on old hatboxes around the shop.

237 STIVALERIA SAVOIA

Via Francesco
Petrarca 7 / Via
Vincenzo Monti
Cairoli-Castello ③
+39 02 463 424
stivaleriasavoia.it

The workshop-studio was 'only' founded in 1925, but their expertise goes back even further, as these shoemakers used to manufacture the boots for the Savoia Cavalry regiment. To this day, they use their savoir faire to produce footwear for sophisticated men, starting with shoes made entirely by hand. Seeing (in the store) is believing.

238 FRANCESCO MAGLIA

Via Ripamonti 194
South-East ⑦
+39 02 5521 9333
francescomaglia.it

The owner, Francesco Maglia, is the fifth generation at the helm of the company. Since 1854, the family has been producing handmade umbrellas, with high-quality materials: natural wood and precious fabrics from Como. They do not come cheap, but this only seems to be an incentive to be more careful and not forget them in the bar as soon as it stops raining.

239 PETRONIUS 1926

Via Elba 22
West ⑥
+39 02 2951 0930
petronius1926.com

This historical name, which is synonymous with excellent craftsmanship and made in Italy, was chosen by the shop's founder, Luigi Wollisch. Today it is proudly brought into the present by his descendants, his son Gastone and his grandchildren Gigliola, Simona and Luigi. They still use their grandfather's scissors to cut ties out of precious fabrics, with patterns that anticipate on trends.

240 ELESTA TRAVEL
VARIOUS TOURS

+39 02 4351 0906
elestatravel.it

The partnership between the Cologni Foundation of Mestieri d'Arte and Elesta Travel, a cultural travel designer, led to the creation of the Milano Grand Tour project. Their aim is to enhance and promote the territory, its traditions and the 'Made in Italy' culture. Follow their itineraries to the workshops of high-end artistic Milanese craftsmanship. They also offer tours dedicated to design, architecture, art, fashion and culture.

VERTICAL FOREST

30 BUILDINGS
TO ADMIRE

———————

5
CHURCHES
you can't afford to miss

---

241 SAN MAURIZIO AL MONASTERO MAGGIORE CHURCH

Corso Magenta 15
Sant'Ambrogio ④
+39 02 8844 5208

The frescoes of the 'Sistine Chapel of Milan' also include Noah's ark with unicorns. This used to be the church of the former Monastero Maggiore, a nunnery founded in the 1500s. The public part was separated from the choir where the nuns sat. The frescoes of the Bernardino Luini school – a magnificent expression of Lombard Renaissance painting – cover the church's walls.

242 BASILICA DI SANT'EUSTORGIO

Piazza
Sant'Eustorgio 1
Ticinese ②
+39 02 5810 1583
+39 02 8940 2671
(museum)
santeustorgio.it

The site of the city's first baptismal font, which was probably built in the 4th century by Bishop Eustorgio. Tradition has it that the relics of the Magi were kept here. They were then stolen by Barbarossa, who destroyed the church. Rebuilt in a Romanesque style, the basilica houses one of the most important examples of the Renaissance in Milan, i.e. the Portinari chapel (1462-1466).

243 SANTA MARIA PRESSO SAN SATIRO CHURCH

Via Torino 17-19
Duomo-San Babila ②
+39 02 874 683

This church was created by combining a 9th-century chapel with the church of Santa Maria, which was built to preserve a 13th-century *Madonna with Child* that was considered miraculous. Today it is known for Donato Bramante's false apse, with its painted perspective of a stucco barrel vault above the main altar.

244 SANCTUARY OF SANTA MARIA ALLA FONTANA

Piazza Santa Maria della Fontana 11
Isola ⑩
+39 02 6887 059

The rich would come here for the healing water of the 'thermal baths outside the walls'. Until the last century the complex was situated in the countryside. It was built by Charles II d'Amboise, the Governor of Milan, for the King of France, who recovered from an eye disease thanks to the water, which was considered miraculous.

245 CHURCH OF SAN BERNARDINO ALLE OSSA

Via Verziere 2
Duomo-San Babila ②
+39 02 7602 3735
sanbernardino alleossa.it

Entirely covered with skulls from the defunct cemeteries, this 17th-century ossuary chapel dedicated to San Bernardino (13th-17th century) is dominated by Sebastiano Ricci's fresco of *The Triumph of Souls and Flying Angels*. Do look at the grate to the *Putridarium*, where the bodies of the friars were left to decompose.

5
LIBRARIES *and* ARCHIVES

246 **BRAIDENSE NATIONAL LIBRARY**
Via Brera 28
Brera-Corso
Garibaldi ①
+39 02 8646 0907
braidense.it

The most important room is dedicated to Archduchess Maria Theresa of Austria, who wanted to open this library to the public in 1786. The walnut wood shelving with the continuous walkway, designed by architect Giuseppe Piermarini, and the 18th-century chandeliers in Bohemian crystal are striking. The latter originally hung in the Palazzo Reale, where they were damaged during WWII.

246 BRAIDENSE NATIONAL LIBRARY

247 CA' GRANDA HISTORICAL ARCHIVE

Via Francesco
Sforza 32
Duomo-San Babila ②
+39 02 9296 5790
vanitasclub.org/archivio

In 2018, Ca' Granda's Historical Archive and Crypt opened to the public. The Archive is a place of extraordinary beauty, with materials that document over 600 years of history. Many Milanese patriots are buried in the Crypt.

248 MAIN PUBLIC LIBRARY OF MILAN

AT: PALAZZO SORMANI
Corso di Porta
Vittoria 6
Duomo-San Babila ②
+39 800 880 066
milano.biblioteche.it

This library has a large reading room with newspapers and magazines. Among the most interesting spaces is the room called '*del Grechetto*', with 23 paintings of the myth of Orpheus taming the animals. But the most enchanting place to read is in the garden at the rear of the building, which is open from April to October.

249 BIBLIOTECA VENEZIA

Via Frisi 2-4
Porta Venezia ⑤
+39 02 8846 5799
milano.biblioteche.it

Behind busy Corso Buenos Aires, there is an open space where a magnolia almost conceals this beautiful art nouveau building from the early 1900s, the old Dumont cinema. Today this neighbourhood library is a good place to read a newspaper or magazine.

250 THE TREES LIBRARY

AT: FONDAZIONE
RICCARDO CATELLA
Via Gaetano de
Castillia 28
Isola ⑩
+39 02 4547 5195
*fondazione
riccardocatella.org*

An open-air library, with trees instead of books. A modern botanic garden, designed by the landscape artist Petra Blaisse, covering 8 hectares under the Porta Nuova skyscrapers. The most unique section is that of the 'vegetable rooms', or circular mini-forests created with single species. There are also meadows and pedestrian and cycling paths.

5
OLD PALAZZOS

251 PALAZZO CLERICI

Via Clerici 5
Duomo-San Babila ②
+39 02 8633 131
ispionline.it

They even organise fashion shows in the gallery of this sumptuous 18th-century palazzo. It's difficult, however, to ignore the vault with frescoes by Tiepolo from 1741, with *The Course of the Chariot of the Sun through the Sky,* which were commissioned by the Clerici family. Now home to the ISPI (Italian Institute for International Political Studies), it can be visited free of charge. Advance booking required.

252 PALAZZO SERBELLONI

Corso Venezia 16
Porta Venezia ①
+39 02 7600 7687
fondazione serbelloni.com

For years, this was the prestigious headquarters of the Press Circle. Today Palazzo Serbelloni, built in 1770, has become an events space, after the Napoleonic layout was carefully altered. You could find yourself sipping a cocktail or dancing among psychedelic lights, in the monumental spaces that welcomed such luminaries as Napoleon Buonaparte, his wife Giuseppina, and Mozart.

253 PALAZZO ISIMBARDI
Via Vivaio 1 /
Corso Monforte 35
Duomo-San Babila ①
+39 02 8845 5555

The building's oldest part dates back to the 16th century and, in addition to serving as the headquarters of the City of Milan, the public can also visit this artistic heritage. The most important artwork is a painting attributed to Giambattista Tiepolo, but the library is also worth visiting as it contains a copy of the *Divine Comedy* by Dante Alighieri illustrated by Amos Nattini.

254 STATE ARCHIVES
AT: PALAZZO DEL SENATO
Via Senato 10
Porta Venezia ①
+39 02 7742 161
archiviodistatomilano.beniculturali.it

From the oldest parchment in Italy to contemporary deeds, scrolls, registers, files, and volumes on approximately 40 kilometres of shelves. Heritage that is preserved in a palace from 1608, which was turned into the state archives after the unification of Italy.

255 PALAZZO LITTA
Corso Magenta 24
Sant'Ambrogio ④

The Mirror Room is 'the best example of 18th-century interior architecture in Milan', with its many mirrors and wood panelling. Napoleon was once received here. On that occasion, Princess Barbara Litta cried a tear on the floor of the 'red living room'. A pearl in the floor still points to this momentous occasion.

5 examples of
MODERNISM

256 CAMPARINO IN GALLERIA
AT: GALLERIA VITTORIO
EMANUELE II
Corner with
Piazza del Duomo
Duomo-San Babila ②
+39 02 8646 4435
camparino.it

This place, which opened in 1915, is the symbol of the aperitif in Milan. At the time, a state-of-the-art hydraulic system in the cellar ensured that guests could always enjoy a cold selzer at the counter. The art nouveau furniture dates from 1923 and was made by the cabinetmaker Eugenio Quarti, the iron craftsman Alessandro Mazzucotelli, and the painter Angiolo d'Andrea. Upstairs you find a new culinary concept by well-known chef Davide Oldani.

257 SHERATON DIANA MAJESTIC
Viale Piave 42
Porta Venezia ⑤
+39 02 20581
*marriott.com/en-us/
hotels/milsi-sheraton-
diana-majestic-milan*

This splendid Liberty-style creation by the architect Achille Manfredini has been transformed into a hotel. Locals love to meet up for drinks in its lovely hidden garden. Originally conceived as Kursaal Diana, it was to include a theatre, a restaurant, a hotel and a pelota court, as well as incorporating 'Diana's Bath', an existing swimming pool (which, unfortunately, could not be preserved).

258 PALAZZO CASTIGLIONI

Corso Venezia 47
Porta Venezia ①

Commissioned at the beginning of the 20th century by the architect Giuseppe Sommaruga, Ernesto Bazzaro's two nude sculptures immediately sparked a scandal, earned the palazzo the nickname 'La Ca' di ciapp' or house of the buttocks. The statues were immediately moved to Villa Faccanoni in Via Buonarroti 48. You can see ironwork by Mazzucotelli inside, including the balustrade and the dragonfly lamp.

259 CASA GALIMBERTI

Via Marcello
Malpighi 3
East ⑥

The art nouveau buildings became a status symbol for the new entrepreneurs. They were eccentric, imaginative, bizarre. The highest concentration of this style can be found in the Porta Venezia area, where Casa Galimberti is also located. The façade features colourful female and male figures, immersed in nature among the vines, winking at passers-by.

260 MONUMENTAL CEMETERY OF MILAN

Piazzale Cimitero
Monumentale
North-West ⑩
+39 02 8844 1274
(tours)

This open-air museum, which opened in 1866, represents the history of the city. There are sculptures and buildings from Realism to Eclecticism, to Art Nouveau – including works by Enrico Butti, Leonardo Bistolfi, Eugenio Pellini, and Adolfo Wildt – and Symbolism. Toscanini, Manzoni, and Quasimodo are buried here. Guided tours upon reservation.

5 examples of
STRANGE ARCHITECTURE

261 **VIA LINCOLN**
East ⑥

Here, the houses are yellow, lilac, green and red. This former working-class neighbourhood from the late 19th century was perhaps intended as a garden city. Today it continues to be a small and colourful corner of Milan. Take a walk among the fruit trees and the small palm trees. Magical.

262 **LE ABBADESSE DI MILANO**
North-West ⑩

A little slice of history of the *Cassin Baess,* as the Milanese call it, which dates from the 11th century. There used to be a convent here and some very old farmhouses, in the countryside. Today only the small church remains, tucked in between modern buildings.

263 **MAGGIOLINA DISTRICT**
North-West ⑩

This residential neighbourhood, with its terraced houses and period buildings, includes some really unique homes, such as the 1970s igloos and a stilt house – a rationalist design by the architect Luigi Figini. In the 1940s, you could also find mushroom-shaped houses here (since demolished), a flight of fancy by an engineer named Cavallé.

264 CA' LONGA

Via Piero della
Francesca 34
North-West ⑩

This used to be the village of the *scigolat*, the greengrocers. This house is a 19th-century farmhouse. It was probably used as a post office, with stables for horses, and was only subsequently transformed into a *casa di ringhiera*, that is a typical Milanese tenement with shared balconies.

265 HOUSES BY TERRAGNI

Isola ⑩

Many examples of 1930s Milanese Rationalism can be found in the Isola neighbourhood, including a design by Giuseppe Terragni. Others include Casa Ghiringhelli (Piazzale Lagosta 2), Casa Comolli-Rustici (Via Guglielmo Pepe 32), near the railway tracks (similar to the one in Corso Sempione, near Via Procaccini) and Casa Toninello (Via Perasto 3), which is also the smallest.

264 CA' LONGA

5 old and new
SKYSCRAPERS

266 VELASCA TOWER
Piazza Velasca 3-5
Porta Romana ②

Studio BBPR's work is no longer that popular nowadays. But for the State, it is 'a world-famous symbol of the architectural rebirth of Milan in the late 20th century'. Perhaps the *Daily Telegraph* did not know this, as it listed one of the greatest expressions of Italian Rationalism as one of the world's ugliest buildings. The Milanese were quite upset.

267 PIRELLI TOWER
Via Fabio Filzi 22
North-East ⑤

Commissioned in 1965 from Giò Ponti, the Pirelli Tower is a concrete structure that 'doesn't rest on a base but emerges, surrounded by a void that separates it from the surrounding low bodies'. Standing 127,10 metres tall, it was the first building to surpass the Duomo and the Madonnina (a statue of the Virgin Mary) in height. For this reason, and as a sign of respect, a Madonnina was installed on top of the tower (a tradition that continues to this day, for each new higher building).

266 VELASCA TOWER

268 VERTICAL FOREST
Via de Castillia /
Via Confalonieri
Isola ⑩

The two towers, designed by Stefano Boeri Architetti, won the 2014 International Highrise Award. The balconies are populated with 800 trees, 4500 bushes and 15.000 plants (which can be replaced but not changed), forming a 2-hectare forest. One of the apartments is listed on Airbnb if you want to spend the night there.

269 CITYLIFE TOWERS
Piazza Tre Torri
West ⑧
city-life.it/it

The Straight, the Twisted, the Curved: they resemble the names of the characters in an old Western. But they are actually the nicknames of three skyscrapers, by Arata Isozaki, Zaha Hadid and Daniel Libeskind respectively. They reach 202, 170 and 175 metres in height, in the redeveloped CityLife district.

270 GALFA TOWER
Via Gustavo Fara 41
North-East ⑤

Featured in Michelangelo Antonioni's movie *La Notte*, the Galfa Tower is a symbol of the Milanese economic boom, which was revamped by BG&K studio. The geometric façade and structure – thirty floors designed by Melchiorre Bega in 1956 – are quite impressive. In 2019 the INNSiDE Milano Torre GalFa opened its doors.

GALLERIA VITTORIO EMANUELE II

60 PLACES TO DISCOVER MILAN

5 beautiful
GARDENS *to admire*

---

271 **BOTANICAL GARDEN OF BRERA**
Via Brera 28
Brera-Corso
Garibaldi ①
+39 02 5031 4683
*ortobotanicoitalia.it/
lombardia/brera*

This tranquil, beautiful oasis is hidden behind the austere Palazzo di Brera, in the centre of Milan. Created in 1774 at the behest of Maria Theresa of Austria, as a haven of pleasure and delight, the Brera Botanical Garden also supplied medicinal plants to the Brera Pharmacy.

272 **BOTANICAL GARDENS OF THE UNIVERSITY**
AT: UNIVERSITY OF MILAN,
FACULTY OF SCIENCE
Via Camillo Golgi 18
East ⑥
+39 02 5032 0886
*ortobotanicoitalia.it/
lombardia/milano*

This space is situated near the Polytechnic University and close to some faculties of the State University. It is open to the public and is used for scientific research and educational activities. Here the region's native species are preserved and studied. The avant-garde green-houses host an interesting collection of carnivorous plants.

273 **ORTI FIORITI AT CITYLIFE PARK**
West ⑧
city-life.it

The CityLife public park will become the city's second 'green lung' and will also have flower gardens. The project includes the cultivation of aromatic and medicinal herbs, flowers and vegetables on 3000 square metres of city land.

274 PARCO TROTTER

Via Giuseppe Giacosa
NoLo ⑤

A former racetrack. In the 1920s Parco Trotter became the *Casa del Sole*, a special school with a state-of-the-art garden with an educational function. Today it's listed as Environmental Heritage and is always teeming with mothers and children who live in this multicultural neighbourhood.

275 ORTICOLA FLOWER SHOW

AT: INDRO MONTANELLI
PUBLIC GARDEN
Corso Venezia
Porta Venezia ①
orticola.org

The opening is always a society event. Guests show off their eccentric hats and colourful clothes, which are all very flowery. It is a pleasure to stroll among the many plant varieties and rare and ancient flowers in the morning when there are fewer people and to stop for a chat with the nursery owners.

271 BOTANICAL GARDEN OF BRERA

5 places to enjoy the
SILENCE

---

276 BASILICA OF SANT'AMBROGIO

Piazza
Sant'Ambrogio 15
Sant'Ambrogio ④
+39 02 8645 0895
*basilica
santambrogio.it*

A masterpiece of the Lombard Romanesque period, which is dedicated to Milan's patron saint, whose remains are kept in a silver urn. It has a gabled façade, brick bell towers and a quadriporticus where pilgrims were welcomed in the past. The frescoes by Gian Battista Tiepolo can be found in the Chapel of San Vittore in Ciel d'Oro.

277 CATHOLIC UNIVERSITY

Largo Gemelli 1
Sant'Ambrogio ④
+39 02 723 41
unicatt.it

Near the Basilica of Sant'Ambrogio there used to be a Benedictine monastery where valuable illuminated manuscripts were produced. Today this building has been transformed into the university's headquarters, while preserving the layout designed by Bramante. Inside there is a garden dedicated to Santa Caterina d'Alessandria, for the exclusive use of female students.

278 CLOISTERS OF THE STATE UNIVERSITY

Via Festa del
Perdono 7
Duomo-San Babila ②
unimi.it

Cà Granda hospital was built by Francesco Sforza in the middle of the 15th century and designed by Filarete (1400–1469). Although it's the main building of the State University (so always full of students), it's always a pleasure to walk around the silent cloisters during lectures and on the weekend. You can see some spectacular installations here during Design Week.

279 LABIRINTO POMODORO

Via Andrea Solari 35
South-West ⑨
+39 02 8907 5394
fondazione
arnaldopomodoro.it

The 'Pomodoro Maze' is a secret and fascinating place, with a long history. Developed in 1995 for an exhibition at the Gió Marconi gallery, it has since been transferred to the former Riva-Calzoni building, then to the site of the Arnaldo Pomodoro Foundation Museum, which is the Fendi showroom today. That is why visits are by reservation only and at scheduled times.

280 BINARIO 21 – MEMORIALE DELLA SHOAH

Piazza Edmond
J. Safra 1
North-East ⑤
+39 02 2820 975
memorialeshoah.it

Situated under Milan's Central Station, Binario 21 refers to the track where trains deported Jews to Nazi concentration camps from 1943 to 1945. Inside, the Shoah Memorial, a wall listing the names of 774 victims, is a place to reflect and contemplate these events.

5 surprising
HOUSE MUSEUMS

281 CASA-MUSEO BOSCHI DI STEFANO

Via Giorgio Jan 15,
2nd Floor
Porta Venezia ⑤
+39 02 7428 1000
fondazione
boschidistefano.it

The home that belonged to Antonio Boschi (1896–1988) and Marieda Di Stefano (1901–1968) is located in an art deco building, designed by the architect Portaluppi. These two great collectors left over 2000 works of 20th-century Italian art, of which 300 are on show, including paintings by Funi, Marussig, Carrà, Casorati, de Chirico and Fontana. Free admission.

282 MUSEUM STUDIO FRANCESCO MESSINA

Via San Sisto 4-A
5vie ②
+39 02 3360 2351
fondazionemessina.it

A place to see dancers frozen in their pose, poetic female busts in polychrome terracotta, plaster, marble and wax, especially in bronze. And drawings, which the Sicilian sculptor Francesco Messina sketched in this special studio. This deconsecrated church in the centre of Milan was almost destroyed during the war and donated to the artist by the municipality in exchange for some of his works.

281 CASA-MUSEO BOSCHI DI STEFANO

283 VILLA NECCHI CAMPIGLIO

Via Mozart 14
Porta Venezia ⓘ
+39 02 7634 0121
*fondoambiente.it/
luoghi/villa-necchi-
campiglio*

Villa Necchi Campiglio is one of the most important examples of a *casa-museo*. Built in the 1930s by Portaluppi, it contains works of immense value, even in the bathroom of the house, dating from the 18th to the 20th century. The garden, one of the first with a swimming pool and a tennis court, also has a bistro bar. A place to enjoy excellent cuisine and silence in the city centre.

284 MUSEO BAGATTI VALSECCHI

Via Gesù 5
Duomo-San Babila ⓘ
+39 02 7600 6132
*museobagatti
valsecchi.org*

The barons and art collectors Fausto and Giuseppe Bagatti Valsecchi lived here. They refurbished the palace in the late 19th century in a neo-Renaissance style. Even today, the atmosphere is quite lively, with coats of arms, coffered ceilings, and artworks, including *Santa Giustina de Borromei* by Giovanni Bellini (1470). They also offer theatrical tours.

285 MUSEO POLDI PEZZOLI

Via Manzoni 12
Duomo-San Babila ⓘ
+39 02 794 889
museopoldipezzoli.it

Here the most fascinating place is the study of the palazzo's former owner, Gian Giacomo Poldi Pezzoli. The most important works in the collection can also be found in the 'Dante cabinet'. But the whole house-museum is full of tapestries, armour, carpets, and wonderful glass. They often organise an aperitivo at the museum.

5 great
SPORTS LOCATIONS

286 COZZI SWIMMING POOL

Viale Tunisia 35
Porta Venezia ⑤
+39 02 6599 703
milanosport.it/
impianto/15/cozzi/27

The Cozzi swimming pool, with its exterior in red brick and marble, was the first indoor pool in Italy and one of the first in Europe, making it an example of cutting-edge technology. Designed and built in 1934 by the engineer Luigi Lorenzo Secchi, it also refers to this historical period with marble floors, inlays and mosaics and a plaque with a warning by Gabriele d'Annunzio to the swimmers.

287 SOCIETÀ DEL GIARDINO

Via San Paolo 10
Duomo-San Babila ②
+39 02 7602 0861
societadelgiardino.it

Established in 1783, the Società del Giardino is one of the world's ten oldest sports clubs. It has a splendid Golden Hall, in a neoclassical style, but its Fencing Room is the real eye-catcher. Engraved in marble are the names of the fencers who contributed to its prestige, like the brothers Edoardo and Dario Mangiarotti. Only upon invitation.

288 CIRCOLO ARCI BELLEZZA

Via Giovanni
Bellezza 16-A
South-East ⑦
+39 02 5831 9492
arcibellezza.it

The gymnasium of Luchino Visconti's 1960 movie, *Rocco and his Brothers*, still exists in the cellar of the Circolo Arci in Via Bellezza and was called the Lombardo gym. The ring, the tools and the scale are all authentic. It will be possibly transformed into a 'gym' for film sets, while preserving the unique setting and the ambience.

289 VELODROMO MASPES-VIGORELLI

Via Arona 19
West ⑧
vigorelli.eu

The legendary Vigorelli, the 'Scala del Ciclismo', was founded in 1935 and has been listed as a structure of historical-artistic interest because of its glorious history. Currently undergoing restoration, the track is open to visitors on rare occasions. The Beatles played their only Italian concert ever here on 24 June 1965.

290 DUOMO DI MILANO

Piazza del Duomo
Duomo-San Babila ②

Why is the biggest Gothic church in Italy, the symbol of the city, included in a chapter dedicated to sport? Because it has more than 2300 statues, carved between the 14th and 20th centuries. There are saints, demons, monstrous animals and famous people, including the boxer Primo Carnera, the first Italian to win the world heavyweight title in 1933.

5 places with
WATER

**291 DRINKING FOUNTAIN
IN PIAZZA SCALA**

Duomo-San Babila ②

There are over 400 drinking fountains in the city. The first, in Piazza Scala, dates from the end of the 1920s and is the only bronze fountain. The others are made of cast iron, painted green, and are dragon-shaped (the Visconti symbol). That's why we also joke: "Let's go to the Green Dragon bar".

**292 FOUNTAIN OF
DE CHIRICO**

AT: PARCO SEMPIONE

Viale Alemagna
Cairoli-Castello ③

triennale.org

Inaugurated in 1973, Giorgio de Chirico's *Bagni Misteriosi* fountain was designed for the gardens of Palazzo dell'Arte, on the occasion of the 15th Triennale. On the occasion of Expo2015, the original colour of the stone figures was restored and they were transferred to the Museo del Novecento. This one, behind La Triennale di Milano, is a copy.

293 BAGNI MISTERIOSI

AT: TEATRO FRANCO
PARENTI

Via Carlo Botta 18
Porta Romana ②
+39 02 8973 1800
bagnimisteriosi.com

The Caimi seaside resort, now called
Bagni Misteriosi (Mysterious Baths), has
resumed operations and has become one
of the most fashionable places in the city.
Designed in the 1930s as a multipurpose
space for fencing and boxing, it was
subsequently expanded with pools.
Today it is a well-maintained monumental
asset and one of the most popular places
to sunbathe and swim in summer. A fun
spot for an evening aperitivo.

294 VICOLO DEI LAVANDAI

Alzaia Naviglio
Grande 14
Porta Genova ⑨

A glimpse of old Milan. Until the 1950s,
men scrubbed clothes in the waters of
the Naviglio here, kneeling on the
brellin (a wooden crate). In the early 20th
century, laundry would be squeezed in
a still visible centrifuge. The term lavandai
(laundry men) reminds us that this was
a man's job. The good old days!

295 QC TERME MILANO

Piazzale Medaglie
d'Oro 2 / Via Filipetti
Ticinese ②
+39 02 5519 9367
termemilano.com

The tall Spanish walls, in the Porta
Romana area, conceal QC Terme, a garden
with a solarium and pools. You'll also
find a Turkish bath, Kneipp baths and
a beautiful bright room with a buffet full
of fresh fruit, yogurt and relaxing herbal
teas in this art nouveau building. The old
tram in the garden is a sauna.

5 interesting places if you're into
FASHION

296 COSTUME MODA IMMAGINE
AT: PALAZZO MORANDO
Via Sant'Andrea 6
Duomo-San Babila ①
+39 02 8846 5735
costumemoda
immagine.mi.it

Palazzo Morando is located in the 'Fashion Quadrilateral', the high-end shopping streets between Via Montenapoleone, Via Manzoni, Via della Spiga and Corso Venezia. A place to showcase and enhance the wealth of clothes and accessories from the past, analyse the image of the present and think of suggestions for the future.

297 THEATRO ALLA SCALA ANSALDO WORKSHOPS
Via Bergognone 34
Porta Genova ⑨
+39 02 4335 3525
teatroallascala.org/en/
ansaldo-workshops

All the Scala Theatre's workshops are located here on the former Ansaldo industrial site: 20.000 square metres of warehouses for crafts (set design, sculpture, carpentry...), costume design and laundry. They also store over 60.000 stage costumes here and there is also a stage space that is identical to the Piermarini stage (La Scala). English tours available.

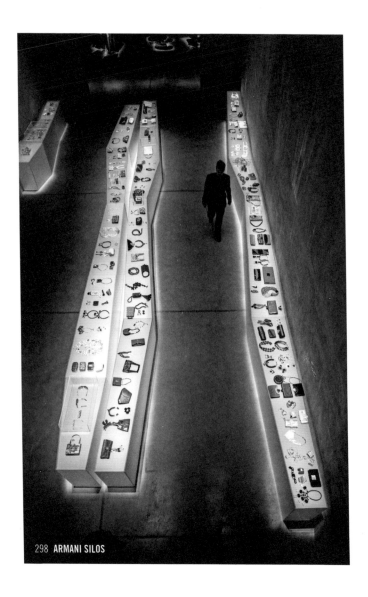

298 ARMANI SILOS

Via Bergognone 40
Porta Genova ⑨
+39 02 9163 0010
armanisilos.com

This former grain silos contain a curated selection of clothes by the fashion brand from 1980 to today on four floors. Sections such as Stars, Daywear, Exotism, Chromatism and Light epitomise the vision of 'King Giorgio' and his timeless aesthetic.

299 MILANO FASHION LIBRARY

Via Alessandria 8
Porta Genova ⑨
+39 02 8331 1211
milanofashionlibrary.it

This library, which originated in a private archive, narrates the history of fashion and clothing from the mid-19th century to the present, with magazines, publications – some very rare, catalogues, and lookbooks. They also have magazines specialised in knitwear, accessories and jewellery. An accessible and searchable collection.

300 APRITIMODA EVENT

apritimoda.it

Made in Italy also means fashion. Visiting the workshops is a unique experience that allows you to appreciate the work of these people, that is synonymous with craftsmanship and culture. An event that invites the public to visit the fashion houses on an autumn weekend. Free admission.

5 must-visit places to learn about
DESIGN

301 FONDAZIONE ACHILLE CASTIGLIONI

Piazza Castello 27
Cairoli-Castello ③
+39 02 8053 606
*fondazione
achillecastiglioni.it*

Welcome to the private world of the designer Achille Castiglioni, who worked in this studio for sixty years. Check out prototypes and models, drafting machines and other curiosities, and walk up to the meeting room, where you'll find the objects that have become part of the history of design.

302 FONDAZIONE FRANCO ALBINI

Via Bernardino
Telesio 13
West ⑧
+39 02 4982 378
*fondazione
francoalbini.com*

This historical archive, which opened to the public in 2007, is the study of one of the most representative figures in Italian and international design and architecture. The itinerary shows where the master worked and tells you more about this important Milanese architect, through 30 of his designs.

303 KARTELL MUSEO

Via delle Industrie 3
Santa Corinna di
Noviglio (suburbs)
+39 02 9001 2269
kartell.com/museo

Inside the Kartell plant, which was founded to celebrate the company's 50th anniversary, the museum occupies a 2500-square-metre area, with a permanent exhibition curated by Ferruccio Laviani, showcasing 1000 iconic objects, from 1949 to the present day. It won the 2000 Guggenheim Award as Best Business Museum. Visits: by appointment only. Free admission.

304 PALAZZO DELLA TRIENNALE

AT: PALAZZO DELL'ARTE
Viale Alemagna 6
Cairoli-Castello ③
+39 02 724 341
triennale.org

This is the headquarters of the Triennale Design Museum, on the first floor of the Palazzo dell'Arte, which was designed in 1933 by Giovanni Muzio for the International Exhibition of Decorative Arts. The exhibitions, talks and encounters with the world of art and design are always quite unique. Creative people love this place, as the exhibition galleries and bookshop always provide fresh inspiration.

305 ADI – THE ASSOCIATION OF INDUSTRIAL DESIGN

Via Bramante 29
North-West ⑩
+39 02 3669 3790
adi-design.org

The Associazione per il Disegno Industriale, which was founded in 1956, awards the 'Compasso d'Oro', the oldest and most prestigious prize in the industry. The complete collection, which was listed by the Ministry of Culture as having artistic and historical interest, has become part of Italy's national heritage and will be exhibited in the new premises, the adjoining former Palazzo Enel, as soon as the restoration is completed.

5 areas to check out during
DESIGN WEEK

---

306 VIA TORTONA

South-West ⑨

tortonadesignweek.com

The area around Via Tortona is the district where the *Fuorisalone* was first organised almost twenty years ago. The event takes place in industrial spaces and is mainly attended by those companies that could not afford to participate in the fair. This spawned a whole series of 'off' events, which are very fashionable today. Many venues host presentations and installations. Keep an eye on Base.

307 NOLO

NoLo ⑤

nolocreativenetwork.it
venturaprojects.com

NoLo (North of Loreto), between Trotter Park and the Martesana Canal, has many unconventional spaces. The large tunnels under the railway tracks of Via Ferrante Aporti – where the Ventura Centrale Project established a temporary location – as well as the former factories, markets, and modern antique stores coordinated by NoLo Creative Network are especially worth checking out.

308 BRERA

Brera-Corso
Garibaldi ①
breradesigndistrict.it

The area where most events take place, due to the many showrooms in the district. Some locations are only open to the public just for the occasion. Or transformed for the Salone, such as Piazzetta San Marco and the patio of the Brera Academy. The buildings on Via Palermo are beautiful and very different from each other: one has medieval interiors, the other a Pelota game room.

309 LE 5VIE

5vie ②
5vie.it

The dialogue between art and design becomes more intimate in Milan's oldest neighbourhood, among strange workshops, fashion shops and an old garage. A walk in Via Santa Marta includes many stops, with courtyard installations, visits to studios, a chat in the doorways of old shops. Do stop at the Cloister of the Humiliated (Chiostre delle Umiliate).

310 ISOLA

Isola ⑩
isoladesigndistrict.com

Even the New York Times wrote up this neighbourhood. Thanks to the Porta Nuova architecture and the new access, it has emerged from its isolation and is becoming increasingly hip. It is home to young designers and emerging international brands, opening its doors to hidden locations including private courtyards and, above all, the many artisan shops.

The 5 best venues to spend your
FREE TIME

---

311 FORMIDABILE LAMBRATE

Via Privata
Giovanni Ventura 3
East ⑥
+39 327 259 1227
*formidabile
lambrate.com*

Pop into Formidabile Lambrate, a cultural association that was established to promote the urban renewal of the district of the same name. Meet up with friends, enjoy a game of table tennis or snack on something in the cafe run by l'Altro Tramezzino. You can also rent an office or share a desk in the coworking area on the first floor.

312 LA SCIGHERA

Via Candiani 131
North-West ⑩
+39 02 4867 1300
lascighera.org

On Tuesdays they organise a folksinging course here; one Sunday a month, they teach Lindy Hop; occasionally 'Viaggi nei Paraggi' trips are organised to discover Milan. And there's also the *scigherina* with games for children. The *scighera,* in dialect, refers the fog, that used to pervade the city during the winter in the old days. Head to the tavern for drinks and good conversation. Open from 6.30 pm onwards.

313 CASCINA MARTESANA

Via Luigi Bertelli 44
North-East ⑤
+39 389 58 20 695
cascinamartesana.com

An old farmhouse transformed into a meeting venue. In the location of Milan's first outdoor pool, you can now explore the El Bagnin de Gorla exhibition space. It is near the Hidden Garden, for yoga and orthotherapy. La Roggia Incantata however is a haven of relaxation, with an open-air lounge and grill, for a picnic with friends. Some activities for members only.

314 SALA VENEZIA

Via Alvise
Cadamosto 2-A
Porta Venezia ⑤
+39 02 2043 765

Dance floors, disco balls, heels and vintage orchestras are fashionable again, even in the centre. Like Sala Venezia, a 'winter' venue (from October to May), where you can dine and dance on Saturdays, while Sundays are for boogie. La Balera dell'Ortica (labaleradellortica.com), in the suburbs, has outdoor spaces and a bowling club. Open all year for dinner, you can dance outdoors here from June to September (Tuesday and Sunday boogie, Thursday swing).

315 BASE

Via Bergognone 34
South-West ⑨
base.milano.it/
casabase

Base is a 'space designed to stimulate creativity and concentration, develop cultural productions and encourage cross-pollination between different disciplines'. It has a workshop, a bistro and some rooms: casaBASE combines the formula of shared rooms with the more classic double rooms with private bathroom. Informal but welcoming.

5 places that are all about
LIGHT

---

316 ALESSIA PALADINI GALLERY
Via Pietro
Maroncelli 11
North-West ⑩
+39 339 712 4519
alessiapaladinigallery.it

In the short time that it's been open, this photo gallery has already carved out a prominent place for itself. Continuing its longstanding collaboration with Contrasto (the most important Italian photo agency), it showcases the work of modern and contemporary photographers, with a special focus on women photographers. The shows, which change every two months, are always interesting as are the vintage and modern works on sale, by Italian and international photographers.

317 OBSERVATORY PRADA
AT: GALLERIA VITTORIO EMANUELE II
Piazza del Duomo
Duomo-San Babila ②
fondazioneprada.org/ visit/milano-osservatorio

Osservatorio Prada questions the cultural and social implications of contemporary photography and visual languages through exhibitions and shows. It is located in the octagon, at the same level of the glass and iron dome that covers the Gallery. The large windows offer a great view. The admission fee includes admission to Fondazione Prada within a 7-day period after your first visit.

318 10 CORSO COMO

Corso Como 10
North-West ⑩
+39 02 653 531
10corsocomo.com

Carla Sozzani's project includes a shop, a bar-restaurant and the hotel rooms in the courtyard of a typical Milanese building, which has since been almost swallowed up by the nearby skyscrapers. The most interesting part is the gallery dedicated to photography, art, design and architecture. From 1990 to the present, it hosted exhibitions of the work of Helmut Newton, Annie Leibovitz, Bruce Weber, Paolo Roversi and David LaChapelle among others.

319 MUSEO FOTOGRAFIA CONTEMPORANEA

AT: VILLA GHIRLANDA
Via Frova 10
Cinisello Balsamo
+39 02 6605 661
mufoco.org

Italy's only public photography museum is located in Villa Ghirlanda, in Cinisello Balsamo and specialises in the conservation, cataloguing, the study and dissemination of photography. It is just outside Milan. Take the subway to Bignami, then tram #31 to Villa Ghirlanda (interurban ticket). Free admission.

320 DIALOGUE IN THE DARK / DIALOGO NEL BUIO

AT: ISTITUTO DEI CIECHI DI MILANO
Via Vivaio 7
Porta Venezia ①
+39 02 7722 6210
dialogonelbuio.org

How do we perceive touch, smell, sound and taste without the sense of sight? The experience, with a visually impaired guide, is to a journey into darkness. Initially you feel as if everything is impossible. Then, unexpectedly, you begin to 'see' things differently.

The 5 most enchanting
S Q U A R E S

---

321 PIAZZA DEI MERCANTI
Duomo-San Babila ②

This medieval square takes its name from the loggia and the arcade that was once used for markets, under the Palazzo della Ragione, the former municipal offices. This is a very old place. On one of the arches, you can find the bas-relief of the 'half-woolly sow', the legendary creature that told the Celtic prince where to found Milan.

322 PIAZZA SANT'ALESSANDRO
5vie ②

In this pedestrian cobbled square you'll feel as if you've left the city. Friends sit on the steps of the Barnabite Church and exchange secrets with the imposing baroque building behind them. The huge church is home to plenty of decoration, frescoes, stuccos, gildings, bas-reliefs.

323 PIAZZA AFFARI
5vie ②

The irreverent work by Maurizio Cattelan, *L.O.V.E.*, stands in the centre of this square. Meaning 'freedom, hatred, revenge, eternity', most people only see a raised middle finger. A vulgar gesture aimed at the financial world? Or a fascist salute, eroded over time, towards Palazzo Mezzanotte and its fascist architecture?

324 GALLERIA VITTORIO EMANUELE II

Duomo-San Babila ②

More than a square, this is the *salotto buono* (the elite hang-out) of Milan, which was inaugurated in 1878 and designed by Giuseppe Mengoni. In 1885 it was illuminated with arc lamps, the first recorded use of electricity in a public space in the world. Don't forget to check out the panoramic route on the Highline Gallery rooftops.

325 PALAZZO LOMBARDIA

Piazza Città di Lombardia 1
Isola ⑩
regione.lombardia.it

Every Sunday morning you can climb to the Belvedere on the 39th floor of Palazzo Lombardia, the headquarters of the Region's offices with a modern covered square, designed by I.M. Pei, the naturalised American Chinese architect and 1983 Pritzker Prize winner. On clear days, you can see the mountains from this 160-metre-high viewpoint. Free admission.

321 **PIAZZA DEI MERCANTI**

5 highly recommended
TOUR GUIDES

326 MILAN GREETERS
milan.greeters.info

A novelty in Milan. They are affiliated with and share the values of the non-profit Global Greeter Network, which was founded 25 years ago in New York and has a presence in more than 150 cities worldwide. They're not tour guides but volunteers who love their city and who want to share their passion with visitors. They don't accept tips.

327 CGM – CENTRO GUIDE TURISTICHE DI MILANO
OFFICE AT:
Piazza Castello 1 /
Via Luca Beltrami
Cairoli-Castello ③
+39 348 566 0758
centroguidemilano.net

The association 'Centro Guide Turistiche di Milano' is composed of certified tour guides. Its members include architects, art historians, archaeologists, and music experts. The tour menu is very diverse and can be themed and customised.

328 NEIADE

OFFICE AT:

Viale Romagna 46
East ⑥
+39 02 3656 5694
neiade.com

There are many ways to see Milan. This company of tour guides – which also organises private tours – stands out because of the experiences they create. Like a picnic at the Sforza Castle, a visit with forensic experts to see the skeletons of the Ca' Granda cemetery, or aperitivos on the roof of the Galleria Vittorio Emanuele II. Night tours also available.

329 ORDINE ARCHITETTI MILANO

OFFICE AT:

Via Solferino 17-19
Brera-Corso
Garibaldi ①
+39 02 625 341
ordinearchitetti.mi.it/
en/mappe/itinerari/
repertorio

These Architecture Itineraries or Architecture Walks in Milan are organised, on specific dates (see website) by the Order of Architect Planners, Landscapers and Conservators of the Province of Milan. A great way to explore the city of Vico Magistretti or Giò Ponti, Milan's new skyscrapers, or the suburbs.

330 IL SIPARIO MUSICALE

OFFICE AT:

Via Molino delle
Armi 11
Ticinese ②
+39 02 5834 941
ilsipariomusicale.com

Specialising in musical tourism, Il Sipario Musicale organises vacations that include the hotel accommodation, opera tickets, concerts, ballets, after-theatre events in historical places, and access to hidden gems. There are special visits to the Ricordi Historical Archive – exclusively for Sipario travellers – for groups.

FONDAZIONE PRADA

60 PLACES TO ENJOY CULTURE

5 ×

LEONARDO DA VINCI

---

331 VIGNA DI LEONARDO
Corso Magenta 65
Sant'Ambrogio ④
+39 02 4816 150
vignadileonardo.com

In front of the church of Maria delle Grazie, where you can see Leonardo Da Vinci's *Last Supper* (*cenacolo.it*), lies the vineyard that Ludovico il Moro, Duke of Milan, gave him in 1498. It has since been replanted with the same grape variety in the original location. Nowadays it's part of the garden of Casa degli Atellani.

332 SALA DELLE ASSE
AT: SFORZA CASTLE
Piazza Castello
Cairoli-Castello ③
+39 02 8846 3703
milanocastello.it

After arriving in Milan in 1482 under the reign of Ludovico il Moro, Leonardo regularly frequented the Sforza Castle. The decoration of the Sala delle Asse (Room of the Wooden Boards) might refer to the Duke himself because of the pergola of mulberry trees that covers the vault.

333 THE AMBROSIAN LIBRARY
Piazza Pio XI 2
Sant'Ambrogio ④
+39 02 806 921
ambrosiana.eu

In 1609, Cardinal Federico Borromeo founded Europe's first public library. It has an amazing collection including Leonardo's *Codex Atlanticus* (dated 1478–1518), arranged in 12 volumes dealing with mathematics, astronomy, botany, and zoology. Here you can also see Leonardo's painting *Portrait of a Musician*.

334 NATIONAL MUSEUM OF SCIENCE AND TECHNOLOGY
Via San Vittore 21
Sant'Ambrogio ④
+39 02 485 551
museoscienza.org

Leonardo was also an inventor, an attentive observer and a keen interpreter of nature. The museum has an installation of 130 three-dimensional models, which were reproduced according to his sketches on paper. There is also an interactive area.

335 CONCA DELL'INCORONATA
Via San Marco
Brera-Corso
Garibaldi ①
naviglilombardi.it

The functioning of the locks, which were part of the ingenious water transportation system that Leonardo invented, can still be seen nowadays at the top of Via San Marco, even though most of it was covered with roads and buildings during the Fascist period. After the restoration, the wooden gates that were used to regulate the flow of water were replaced.

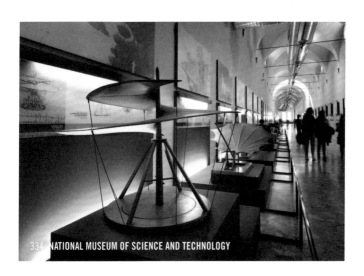

334 NATIONAL MUSEUM OF SCIENCE AND TECHNOLOGY

5 places for fans of
GIUSEPPE VERDI

---

336 LA SCALA THEATRE AND MUSEUM

Largo Ghiringhelli 1,
Piazza Scala
Duomo-San Babila ②
+39 02 8879 7473
museoscala.org
teatroallascala.org

Verdi made his debut at La Scala in 1839. His *Nabucco* premiered at the Piermarini in 1842. The museum has several interesting exhibits, such as a cast of his right hand and some paintings: a severe Verdi portrait by Achille Scalese and paintings of his wives, Margherita Barezzi and Giuseppina Strepponi. The visit includes both the theatre and the museum.

337 GRAND HOTEL ET DE MILAN

Via A. Manzoni 29
Brera-Corso
Garibaldi ①
+39 02 723 141
grandhoteletdemilan.it

This was once called Albergo di Milano and the Maestro stayed in suite 105, his 'home' when he was in town. The Milanese worshipped him to such an extent that when he fell ill they asked for the medical bulletins to be published. They covered the street with straw and wrapped the horses' hooves in cloth to prevent noise nuisance. Verdi died here on 27 January 1901.

338 PASTICCERIA COVA

Via Monte-
napoleone 8
Duomo-San Babila ①
+39 02 7600 5599
covamilano.com

Today this pastry shop, which was founded in 1817, is part of the LVMH international fashion group but originally it was a literary cafe, a meeting place for intellectuals, the bourgeoisie, and patriots during the Risorgimento. Also frequented by Verdi, who had his favourite table. The precious furnishings, crystal chandeliers, mirrors and polychrome floors have all been preserved.

339 SAN MARCO CHURCH

Piazza San Marco 2
Brera-Corso
Garibaldi ①

Verdi did not attend Alessandro Manzoni's funeral, although they were good friends. He did however compose the famous *Messa da Requiem* for him. A year after his death, he directed a moving performance of his composition in the Church of San Marco. This religious building, a Latin cross plan with three naves, has impressive dimensions. There is also a football pitch in the cloister.

340 CASA VERDI

Piazza Buonarroti 29
West ⑧
+39 02 4996 009
casaverdi.it

Verdi said that his retirement home for musicians was 'his most beautiful work'. The Gothic building that the master of Busseto designed with Camillo Boito accommodates 'people involved in the musical arts who live in poverty'. It is also where the Master and his second wife Giuseppina Strepponi are buried. The crypt can be visited from 8.30 am to 6 pm.

5 tips for
CLASSICAL MUSIC

---

341 ASSOCIAZIONE MUSICALE ARTEVIVA
VARIOUS LOCATIONS
+39 02 3675 6460
*associazione
arteviva.com*

The Arteviva Chamber Orchestra has been active for almost 20 years, with a repertoire ranging from Viennese classical works to compositions by contemporary authors, under conductor Matteo Baxiu. They give concerts in the splendid setting of the Basilica of Santa Maria delle Grazie.

342 SOCIETÀ DEL QUARTETTO
VARIOUS LOCATIONS
+39 02 795 393
quartettomilano.it

This society organises one of the most important chamber concerts seasons in Europe since 1864, when the composer Arrigo Boito and the editor Tito Ricordi lobbied for the 'constitution of a music academy to be called Quartet Society'. Some concerts are held in the Giuseppe Verdi retirement home.

343 SERATE MUSICALI
+39 02 2940 9724
seratemusicali.it

Forty years of history and a very busy programme. Many of the artists they have invited to Milan have since become international stars, such as Hilary Hahn, Piotr Anderszewski, Yevgeny Sudbin, and Leonidas Kavakos. Others are sure to follow in their footsteps because the Serate Musicali (Musical Evenings) have traditionally featured some of the greatest international musicians, as well as presenting very young talent.

344 I POMERIGGI MUSICALI
AT: TEATRO DAL VERME
Via San Giovanni sul Muro 2
Cairoli-Castello ③
+39 02 879 05
ipomeriggi.it

Founded in 1945, this project combines a classical repertoire with contemporary compositions. Since the very start, this event has contributed to the dissemination of leading 20th-century composers, although it was censored by the Fascists. Today the vast repertoire includes Baroque, Classicism, early Romanticism, modern and contemporary music. Hosted at the Dal Verme Theatre.

345 LAVERDI
+39 02 8338 9401
laverdi.org

Established by the Russian conductor Vladimir Delman and the direcor Luigi Corbani, this has proven to be one of the most appreciated symphonic orchestras, both nationally and internationally, in the past 20 years. Its repertoire spans from the 1700s to contemporary compositions. Most concerts are held at the Milan Auditorium.

5 venues for
JAZZ LOVERS

---

346 MASADA

**Viale Carlo
Espinasse 41
North-West** ⑩
masadamilano.it

Masada is a welcoming cultural association, which is very popular with musicians because it has an interesting programme. Musicians play in a small garage that has been furnished with discarded material, including tables and cinema chairs. Behind the stage there is also a bookshop. Sunday is the most interesting evening. No need to book.

347 CLIVATI 1969

**Viale Coni Zugna 57
Porta Genova** ⑨
+39 02 8322 591
pasticceriaclivati.com

Jazz in a pastry shop? Yes, one night a week – check the Facebook page for dates – the small room hosts intimate concerts. An aperitif (and maybe dinner) with music, to match with savoury pastries and a cocktail made with Italian vermouth: Milanese-style *cannoli*, carbonara beignet, *cacio e pepe cannoncino*… Clivati is a Milan institution and a favourite bakery on Instagram.

348 **BACHELITE CLAB**
Via Vertoiba 3
South-East ⑦
+39 340 8919 707

Off the beaten path, this is one of those places where musicians like to come together for impromptu jam sessions. The former car workshop has been renovated, combining post-industrial design with modern furnishings and Bakelite objects. Drop in on Wednesdays.

349 **JAZZ BAR ALLO SMERALDO**
AT: EATALY SMERALDO
Piazza Venticinque Aprile 10
North-West ⑩
+39 347 325 5558
eataly.net/it_it/negozi/ milano-smeraldo/news/ jazz-bar-allo-smeraldo

Anything from contemporary to mainstream jazz, folk music and funky jazz, fusion and chamber music. Jazz Bar allo Smeraldo has a spring programme, which brings some of the greatest names as well as new and interesting musical projects to the Eataly stage.

350 **NORD EST CAFÈ**
Via Pietro Borsieri 35
Isola ⑩
+39 02 6900 1910

A place that has been somewhat overshadowed by its neighbour – the Blue Note. Even though Nord Est is older and has maintained a more easy-going atmosphere. Every Thursday evening there's live music, with emerging and established Milanese jazz musicians. Nord Est also has a small outdoor space.

5 acclaimed
THEATRES

351 TEATRO STUDIO MELATO

Via Rivoli 6
Cairoli-Castello ③
+39 02 4241 1889
piccoloteatro.org

Originally founded as an experimental space for drama students, the 19th-century Teatro Fossati, now called the Teatro Studio Melato, is the smallest theatre of the Piccolo Teatro di Milano, which was founded by Strehler, Grassi and Vinchi in 1947. Directors love it best however. The other theatres are Teatro Strehler (Largo Grappi 1) and Teatro Grassi (Via Rovello 2), near the restored renaissance cloister, with a bookshop and bar. Excellent aperitivo.

352 TEATRO DEI FILODRAMMATICI

Via Filodrammatici 1
Duomo-San Babila ②
+39 02 3672 7550
teatrofilodrammatici.eu

Although this theatre was built in 1798 by the architect Luigi Canonica after sketches by Piermarini in the deconsecrated church of San Damiano alla Scala, its exterior is more Art Nouveau (early 20th century). Since 2010, the Accademia dei Filodrammatici (which also managed it in the early 19th century) has been in charge, offering a very interesting contemporary programme.

353 MANIFATTURE TEATRALI MILANESI

Corso Magenta 24
Sant'Ambrogio ④
+39 02 8055 882
mtmteatro.it

The Manifatture Teatrali Milanesi project is the result of the merger of two theatrical entities that operated in the area for 40 years: Teatro Litta and the Quelli di Grock Cooperative. Keep an eye on the programme, because it combines a passion for a new approach with socially engaged theatre and education.

354 TEATRO GEROLAMO

Piazza Cesare
Beccaria 8
Duomo-San Babila ②
+39 02 4538 8221
teatrogerolamo.it

'A veritable treasure chest'. That is what the artistic director, Roberto Bianchin, who also is a consultant of the Fenice in Venice, calls this theatre, which returned to the city after thirty years. Built in 1868 as the first European venue specifically designed for puppet theatre, the 209-seat pretty theatre has been beautifully restored.

355 TEATRO BRUNO MUNARI

LA CASA DEL TEATRO
DEL BURATTO
Via Giovanni Bovio 5
North-West ⑩
+39 02 2700 2476
teatrodelburatto.it

This theatre, in the former 'industrial citadel' of the Carlo Erba pharmaceutical company, spans three floors and was designed by the architect Italo Rota. Inside you'll find a large foyer, the theatre itself and spaces for educational activities and games.

5 fascinating stops for
CONTEMPORARY ART

356 **FABBRICA DEL VAPORE**

Via G. C. Procaccini 4
North-West ⑩
fabbricadelvapore.org

A 30.000-square-metre space, that is half covered and is dedicated to all artforms including visual, performative and multimedia. The Fabbrica is situated in premises that once belonged to a railway equipment factory, with sheds, buildings with large windows and an art nouveau design, where young artists can also reside. Check the online events calendar.

357 **FONDAZIONE PRADA**

Largo Isarco 2
South-East ⑦
+39 02 5666 2611
fondazioneprada.org

Rem Koolhaas's OMA studio has juxtaposed the existing buildings of an early-20th-century distillery with three new buildings, called Podium, Cinema and Tower. The latter, which was inaugurated in 2018, offers an unprecedented view of the city through the large windows and from the rooftop bar. All the spaces host artworks and installations from the Prada collection.

358 PIRELLI HANGARBICOCCA

358 PIRELLI HANGARBICOCCA

Via Chiese 2
North-East ⑤
+39 02 6611 1573
pirellihangarbicocca.org

The Seven Heavenly Palaces – towers of concrete and rubble that reach lopsided for the sky inside a semi-dark hangar – are a poetic artwork by the artist Anselm Kiefer and a reason to 'escape' the city, and head to this former industrial area. The programme of this contemporary arts laboratory always includes interesting exhibitions.

359 SANTA MARIA ANNUNCIATA IN CHIESA ROSSA CHURCH

Via Neera 24
Abbiategrasso (MI)
South-West ⑨

Designed by Giovanni Muzio in 1930, this church houses a light installation by the artist Dan Flavin, who belongs to the minimalist movement. The artwork, which was inaugurated in 1997, is also the American artist's last work, filling the space with a chromatic progression of colours. Hours: 4 pm to 7 pm. Free admission.

360 SAN FEDELE MUSEUM

AT: SAN FEDELE CHURCH
Piazza San Fedele 4
Duomo-San Babila ②
+39 02 863 521
sanfedeleartefede.it

Classic artworks stand alongside more contemporary pieces. The church houses works by Lucio Fontana (*Via Crucis*), Pietro Manzoni (*Pressure*), Jannis Kounellis (*Crucifixion*), Hidetoshi Nagasawa (*Boat*) and photographer Joel Meyerowitz (*Provincetown*). The Madonna painting in the so-called Ballerina's Chapel, where the étoiles of the Scala came to light a candle before performing, is more classical.

5
CONTEMPORARY ART GALLERIES

---

361 **MASSIMO DE CARLO**
   Viale Lombardia 17
   East ⑥
   +39 02 7000 3987
   massimodecarlo.com

Massimo De Carlo's third gallery opened in 2019. After Via Ventura, in the Lambrate area, and Piazza Belgioioso, in the 18th-century building designed by Piermarini, he now restored a building designed by Piero Portaluppi in the 1930s, i.e. Casa Corbellini-Wassermann in Viale Lombardia. Another elegant contemporary art gallery.

362 **FRANCESCA MININI**
   Via Privata
   Massimiano 25
   East ⑥
   +39 02 2692 4671
   francescaminini.it

Francesca, the daughter of the gallery owner Massimo Minini, sells the work of emerging Italian and international artists. Her gallery, in the Ventura area, is a white cube and opened in 2006. She represents such artists as Flavio Favelli, Giulio Frigo and Riccardo Previdi.

363 LIA RUMMA

Via Stilicone 19
North-West ⑩
+39 02 2900 0101
liarumma.it

This structure on three floors, with a terrace, in a suburban area, has become the place to be since 2000, and is owned by the Neapolitan Lia Rumma. She represents several prominent artists, from Marina Abramović to Vanessa Beecroft and Anselm Kiefer, as well as a few Italian proponents of contemporary art.

364 ARTESPRESSIONE

Via della Palla 3
5vie ②
artespressione.com

Paula Nora Seegy opened her space in May 2009 in Old Milan. Her intention is to create interactions between various artistic expressions – painting, sculpture, and photography – hosting exhibitions and events. The curator, Matteo Pacini, puts together an exhibition programme with an international flavour.

365 FUTURDOME

Via Giovanni
Paisiello 6
East ⑥
+39 393 4040 233
futurdome.com

It's been called a 'museum housing project dedicated to contemporary art'. This experiment aims to reclaim the existing building heritage with a combination of conservative restoration, technology, and artistic interventions. In an art nouveau building that was the meeting place of the Futurists in the 1940s.

5 masterpieces to see at the
PINACOTECA
DI BRERA

---

366 LA PINACOTECA DI BRERA

Via Brera 28
Brera-Corso
Garibaldi ①
+39 02 722 631
pinacotecabrera.org

With the help of director James Bradburne, who in recent years has redesigned all 38 rooms, the Pinacoteca di Brera has become even more attractive and lively. Examples of this are some new activities, such as the music sessions held on every third Thursday of the month, with young musicians from the Claudio Abbado School of Music.

367 THE MARRIAGE OF THE VIRGIN

By Raphael

An early work by Raphael – he painted it in 1504, following the composition and the iconography of a similar painting by Perugino, with whom he trained. The student became the master over time. The temple, with its converging perspective lines, becomes the centre of the scene, while the figures have been arranged in a semicircle to underscore the geometric and formal perfection of the architecture.

368 PIETÀ
By Giovanni Bellini

This *Pietà* is moving because of the great humanity of its figures and the emotional impact of the Virgin's pained expression as she gazes at her son. A characteristic of the subsequent works of the artist, who was Mantegna's brother-in-law and who, like him, liked to place figures in the foreground. It is dated between 1465–70.

369 SUPPER AT EMMAUS
By Caravaggio

A previous version exists, which is exhibited at the National Gallery in London. The Brera painting (1605–1606) was created after Caravaggio fled Rome where he had been convicted of murder. The use of *chiaroscuro,* which highlights the most realistic details and Christ's melancholic face, makes this painting so beautiful.

370 THE LAMENTATION OF CHRIST
By Andrea Mantegna

The striking image of Christ covers almost all of the canvas and, because of the use of trompe l'oeil, draws us into the painting, as if we have become part of the group of mourners gathered around the body. Belonging to the Gonzaga family, this was acquired by the portrait gallery in 1824. It is one of the symbols of the Italian Renaissance.

5

ARCHITECTURAL LANDMARKS

---

371 **ARCHAEOLOGICAL MUSEUM**

Corso Magenta 15
Sant'Ambrogio ④
+39 02 8844 5208
museoarcheologico milano.it

Located in the former convent of the Monastero Maggiore of San Maurizio, which was founded in the 8th century, this archaeological museum is a great place to see traces of the great Roman circus adjacent to the imperial palace, which dates from the late 3rd century. A new app also allows you to take a virtual tour inside the Roman towers and among the museum's works.

372 **THE CRYPT OF THE HOLY SEPULCHRE**

Piazza San Sepolcro
5vie ②
+39 02 9296 5790
vanitasclub.org/ cripta-di-san-sepolcro

The crypt that was built in 1030 at the crossing of Cardo and Decumaus of the ancient *Mediolanum* attracts very few visitors, because it reopened just a couple of years ago. Dedicated to the Knights of the Holy Sepulchre, upon their return from the first crusade to Jerusalem, the crypt has retained its original floor and the 14th-century frescoes. The restoration is financed with ticket sales. Booking online is free and recommended.

373 ROMAN FORUM

Piazza Pio XI 2
5vie ②
+39 02 806 921
ambrosiana.it

The ancient *Mediolanum* was one of the main centres of the Roman Empire and had a forum of which many traces remain. Over the centuries, emperors, illustrious men and saints, such as Ambrose, the patron saint of Milan, walked along the main avenue. Thursdays and Fridays 'Roman aperitif' for 15 euro.

374 AMPHITEATRUM VIRIDANS

Via de Amicis
Sant'Ambrogio ④
architettonicimilano.
lombardia.
beniculturali.it

A very special project is being developed in this area, to be completed in the next three years. Box, laurel, myrtle and cypress trees will retrace the elliptical profile of the Roman amphitheatre, which was built in the first half of the first century AD, of which traces remain in the archaeological area in Via de Amicis. The theatre, which was 155 metres long and 125 metres wide, could seat 35.000 people.

375 ETRUSCAN MUSEUM

AT: PALAZZO BOCCONI-
RIZZOLI-CARRARO
Corso Venezia 52
Porta Venezia ⑤
fondazioneluigi
rovati.org/il-museo-
di-arte-etrusca

The Etruscan Museum extends beneath the gardens of the Palazzo Bocconi-Rizzoli-Carraro. It reopened in May 2022 after a major renovation, and will house the new restaurant of two Michelin-starred chef Andrea Aprea.

The 5 most interesting
CINEMAS

---

376 CINEMA BELTRADE
Via Nino Oxilia 10
NoLo Ⓜ
+39 02 2682 0592
cinemabeltrade.net

The former cinema of the Church of Santa Maria Beltrade has become an institution for fans of experimental cinema, because it screens films from international festivals and cult movies. In the middle of the up-and-coming NoLo neighbourhood.

377 CINEMA CENTRALE
Via Torino 30-32
5vie Ⓜ
+39 02 874 826
multisalacentrale.it

When it opened in 1907, it was called Mondial and it was the first proper multiplex in Italy. The two cinemas, with vaulted ceilings, are situated inside the 15th-century Palazzo Grifi, in which Leonardo may have lived. Mostly arthouse.

378 FONDAZIONE CINETECA ITALIANA – SPAZIO OBERDAN
Viale Vittorio Veneto 2 /
Piazza Oberdan
Porta Venezia Ⓜ
+39 02 8398 2421
cinetecamilano.it/ films/spazio-oberdan

Inside the building renovated by architect Gae Aulenti, you'll find the main hall of the Fondazione Cineteca Italiana, with 200 seats. It organises numerous film festivals, screenings with directors, previews and cult movies. You'll need a membership card plus a ticket to attend screenings.

379 CINEMA MEXICO

Via Savona 57
South-West ⑨
+39 02 4895 1802
cinemamexico.it

The Mexico is famous for *The Rocky Horror Picture Show,* Jim Sharman's cult classic from 1975. This cinema has been screening it nonstop since 1976. From the eighties onwards, imitating the trends in the States, a performance group of amateur actors re-enacts what happens in the film with the audience joining in. Always fun.

380 CINEMINO

Via Seneca 6
Porta Romana ②
+39 02 3594 8722
ilcinemino.it

Check out this cinema club, which screens arthouse films, animation, documentaries and unreleased films (members only) as well as short films, videoclips and new forms of audiovisuals. All in the original language with multi films in one evening, followed by a debate, possibly in the cosy traditional bar, which is open to everyone.

5 places for must-see
EXHIBITIONS

---

381 ROYAL PALACE

Piazza del Duomo 12
Duomo-San Babila ②
+39 02 8844 5181
palazzorealemilano.it

Palazzo Reale (Royal Palace) has been the seat of the city's government for centuries and is an essential part of its history. The 1943 bombings proved fatal for the large Salone delle Cariatidi, which remained roofless and at the mercy of the elements for many years. This also explains why Picasso showed his *Guernica* here ten years later. Since then the building has become a major exhibition venue.

382 GAM – MODERN ART GALLERY OF MILAN

Via Palestro 16
Porta Venezia ①
+39 02 8844 5943
gam-milano.com

The GAM building (Galleria di Arte Moderna), which was designed by Leopoldo Pollack at the end of the 18th century, is one of the masterpieces of Milanese Neoclassicism. Since 1921 it's hosted modern art exhibitions, starting from Neoclassicism, with Canova and Hayez, moving on to Romanticism, right up to the Scapigliatura and Divisionism. You can also visit the Grassi Collection here, with works by Manet, Cézanne, Van Gogh, and Gauguin.

384 MUSEO DEL NOVECENTO

383 GALLERIE D'ITALIA

Piazza della Scala 6
Duomo-San Babila ②
+39 800 167 619
gallerieditalia.com

The home of the Intesa Sanpaolo banking group's art treasures. In the basement of the former hall of the Banca Commerciale Italiana, a large vault, which was transformed by the architect De Lucchi into a warehouse, is home to several artworks which you can see through a metal gate. Occasional guided tours available.

384 MUSEO DEL NOVECENTO

AT: PALAZZO
DELL'ARENGARIO
Piazza del Duomo
Duomo-San Babila ②
+39 02 8844 4061
museodelnovecento.org

Designed by Griffini, Magistretti, Muzio and Portaluppi and renovated by the Rota Group in 2010, the Palazzo dell'Arengario is home to 4000 pieces of 20th-century Italian art. A scenic spiral ramp connects the galleries, leading to Pellizza da Volpedo's *The Fourth Estate*. A fascinating journey that ends with Lucio Fontana's *Neon*.

385 PAC – PADIGLIONE D'ARTE CONTEMPORANEA

Via Palestro 14
Porta Venezia ①
+39 02 8844 6359
pacmilano.it

On the perimeter of the former Royal Palace Stables (GAM headquarters), which were bombed during WWII, the architect Ignazio Gardella created a museum space in 1955, that connects with the park through a large window. Today it is one of Milan's most interesting spaces for art and photography exhibitions.

5
CULTURAL EVENTS
you won't want to miss

386 **MIART**
AT: FIERAMILANOCITY,
PAV. 3, GATE 5
Viale Scarampo
West ⑧
miart.it

The international modern and
contemporary art fair, in March, is
a prestigious showcase for 200 galleries
from 18 different countries and an
important meeting opportunity for
curators and museum directors. Miart
also organises Art Week, across the entire
city with galleries open on the weekend.

387 **PIANO CITY MILANO**
VARIOUS LOCATIONS
pianocitymilano.it

A weekend in May, which is dedicated to
piano music throughout the city. From
middle-class apartments to hotel halls,
from the frescoed galleries of museums
to even the trams. With plenty of classical
and contemporary music concerts in
parks, where people sunbathe as they
enjoy the music. Two days of workshops,
improvisations and concerts. Some events
require booking.

388 MITO SETTEMBREMUSICA
VARIOUS LOCATIONS
mitosettembre musica.it

In September, Milan and Turin create a 'single stage' for a programme of classical music concerts by internationally-renowned artists. A special month for fans and newbies to learn more about music. Many performances are for children and teenagers. At affordable prices.

389 JAZZMI
VARIOUS LOCATIONS
jazzmi.it

More music, in September, during an event that immediately won over the public. The high-quality programme includes concerts by world-famous jazz icons and emerging artists, who present new musical languages. Performances in theatres, clubs, concert halls and art galleries.

390 MILANO FILM FESTIVAL
VARIOUS LOCATIONS
+39 02 5401 9076
milanofilmfestival.it

An 11-day-long movie marathon is the highlight of the Milanese autumn. From the end of September, the Milano Film Festival brings the best of Italian and international independent cinema to the screen. The festival takes place at the Base Milano, Mudec and Ducale Multisala, where directors, film buffs and fans gather.

GARDEN OF VILLA BELGIOJOSO

25 PLACES
FOR CHILDREN

———

5 fun places in the
OPEN AIR

---

391 GARDEN OF VILLA BELGIOJOSO
AT: VILLA REALE
Via Palestro 8
Porta Venezia ①
gam-milano.com/en/
villa/garden

Only adults (accompanied by children) can enter the English garden of Villa Reale. Near today's playground, you'll find a pond that was designed at the end of the 18th century in such a way that it was never possible to see all of it, a ploy that fuelled the imagination. The botanic path is also beautiful.

392 PEREGO GARDEN
Via dei Giardini 6
Brera-Corso
Garibaldi ①

Milan's smallest and most central park. Quiet and suitable for a walk with the pram or for children to play. Designed by Luigi Canonica at the end of the 18th century for the Perego family of Cremnago. He annexed the gardens of Sant'Erasmo Monastery, after which it was transformed into an English garden by the head gardener Luigi Villoresi, who also oversaw the garden at the Royal Villa in Monza.

393 GARDENS INDRO MONTANELLI

Corso Venezia
Porta Venezia ①

A rattling train, roundabouts, games. Large avenues to ride your bike and a bar, where you can stop for a snack and a yoghurt. Older boys stretch out with elastic bands and do acrobatics in the meadows, enjoy a picnic or sunbathe. Designed in the late 1700s with a French layout, this is the city's first public park, which is very popular with the Milanese.

394 BOSCOINCITTÀ PARK
AT: CASCINA SAN ROMANO

Via Novara 340
West ⑧
+39 02 4522 401
boscoincitta.it

Boscoincittà surrounds a 15th-century house and has arcades for parties and barbecues, protected areas for children to play, vegetable gardens, as well as shrubs, trees, flowers, and spontaneous vegetation. A 110-hectare park, and the city's first example of urban reforestation, the park is managed by the Italia Nostra association.

395 FRUTTA IN CAMPO
AT: PARCO SUD

Via Caio Mario
West ⑧
fruttaincampo.it

Grab a basket, take a stroll, gather some fruit and pay at the exit. They call it 'pick your own' and it became hugely successful thanks to a field of 350.000 tulips on the outskirts of Milan. Now the city orchard applies the same concept. Covering a surface area of 2,5 hectares you can pick apricots, apples, plums, pears and cherries from the 2000 trees here. All organic and seasonal, of course.

5 cute
SHOPS FOR KIDS

396 **LE CIVETTE SUL COMÒ**
Via Vittorio Salmini 4
South-East ⑦
+39 02 4548 0697
lecivettesulcomo.com

Furnishing your children's bedroom and game station has never been so easy. Here they sell furniture, chairs and ottomans, tables and desks, and containers for everything. Last but not least, mums will love the cute and fun objects to brighten up the table.

397 **CROCHETTE**
Corso Garibaldi 44
Brera-Corso
Garibaldi ①
+39 02 3674 3845
crochette.it

A workshop for children, established by a mother and daughter, Marvi Castagna and Cristiana Seassaro. Marvi has years of experience in the textile industry, while stylist Cristiana has a degree in architecture and a passion for design. She also has three in-house 'models' (her children), a boy and twin girls.

398 TEO LAB

Via Carlo Goldoni 57
East ⑥
+39 02 9925 0238

At Teo, everything is handmade, without a logo. He's always on the lookout for artisans, working with Italian and sometimes even foreign brands to find interesting stuff. He also produces a lot in house, including knitwear and nursery accessories. They also make clothes to order.

399 DOUUOD

Via Mercato 8
Brera-Corso
Garibaldi ①
+39 02 8909 5093
douuodkids.com

A comfortable, casual, practical style, with soft fabrics such as fleece, jersey and cotton, and neutral and dusty colours. All made in Italy, and reflecting the style and sensibility of the designer, Elisabetta Mambelli, who always pays attention to shapes and volumes – very contemporary – as well as comfort. Also an online shop.

400 MATIA'S BABY OUTLET

Via Eugenio Balzan 2
Brera-Corso
Garibaldi ①
+39 02 6208 7881
matiasfashionoutlet.
wordpress.com

Over 300 square metres of designer clothing for mini fashionistas under the vaulted ceilings of a building in the central Brera area. Browse the racks for everyday items as well as clothes and accessories for more formal and even ceremonial occasions. Simply irresistible miniature clothes (and shoes!) for your little ones.

5 interactive and never-boring
MUSEUMS

---

401 MUBA – MUSEO DEI BAMBINI

Via Enrico Besana 12
East ⑥
+39 02 4398 0402
muba.it

Interactive exhibitions, workshops for where material is creatively recycled, cultural and artistic activities for children. The Children's Museum, the 18th-century complex of the Rotonda della Besana (a former church), also has a bookshop, curated by Corraini, and a cafeteria.

402 MUSEO CIVICO DI STORIA NATURALE

Corso Venezia 55
Porta Venezia ⑤
+39 02 8846 3337

The best galleries are those with the dinosaur skeletons and the full-size reconstruction of a triceratops. But the museum itself is also a fascinating place, an eclectic building with 23 halls and 3 million exhibits, in the galleries and depot. A vintage setting with cutting-edge children's workshops.

403 ACQUARIO CIVICO MILANO

Viale Gerolamo
Gadio 2
Cairoli-Castello ③
+39 02 8846 5750
acquariocivico
milano.eu

This is not just a museum for children, even if there are guided tours, workshops and learning opportunities that were especially designed for them. An itinerary to explore the world of water, the creatures that populate it, and how to respect it. A passion they share with the naturalists and biologists.

404 NATIONAL MUSEUM OF SCIENCE AND TECHNOLOGY

Via San Vittore 21
Sant'Ambrogio ④
+39 02 4855 51
www.museoscienza.org

You can enter the submarine, the S-506 Enrico Toti in the museum. Or see a fragment of a moon rock collected during the Apollo mission, and the legendary AC72 Luna Rossa catamaran from the America's Cup. But children are the stars here every week, with guides ready to answer the most wide-ranging questions. The topics? Human beings, food, means of transportation and robotics.

405 MUDEC – MUSEUM OF CULTURE

Via Tortona 56
South-West ⑨
+39 02 549 17
mudec.it

Children become little explorers, with a notebook and pencil to take notes, answer quizzes and learn by playing, in galleries that preserve ethno-anthropological heritage, with artworks, objects, fabrics and tools from all continents. A tour of the world that continues in the museum's depots, which can be visited. A fun discovery for adults, too.

404 NATIONAL MUSEUM OF SCIENCE AND TECHNOLOGY

5 cool things to do for
LITTLE ARTISTS

406 UNDUETRESTELLA
Via Gian Battista
Vico 1
Sant'Ambrogio ④
+39 02 8945 2445
unduetrestellababy.com

No set programme. Unduotrestella — the name of a playground game — is an experimental workshop for young children, that always invents innovative links between creativity and art. They often organise workshops during important events, such as the Salone del Mobile or Triennale.

407 L'ARTÈ
AT: LABORATORIO
DELLE ARTI
Via Bergognone 7
South-West ⑨
+39 02 4398 0151
laboratoriodellearti.org

Brushes, colours and paper: these are just some of the tools that Valeria Giunta uses in her artistic workshop, to allow children and teenagers to express their creativity, while being inspired by important artists such as Matisse, Kandinsky and Klee. On Saturdays there are artistic workshops. Some family workshops are also available in English.

408 ATELIER CARLO COLLA & FIGLI

Via Montegani 35/1
South-East ⑦
+39 02 8953 1301
marionettecolla.org

The performances of Atelier Carlo Colla & Figli, the famous puppeteers, continue! They organise educational activities and workshops to introduce children and teens to the world of puppets. Check the website!

409 MUSEO DEL FUMETTO

AT: GIARDINO ORESTE DEL BUONO
Viale Campania 12
East ⑥
+39 02 4952 4744
museowow.it

The former headquarters of Motta (who make Panettone, the famous Milanese dessert) are now populated by fictional characters loved by both children and adults alike, among whom many artists, publishers, and *fumetti* enthusiasts. On Sunday afternoons the museum hosts workshops on stop-motion drawing and animation. You can learn about the origins of Manga, create superhero costumes, or draw with other children. They also organise comic-book-themed parties.

410 RADIOMAMMA

radiomamma.it

'Radiomamma' is one of the most popular sites for mothers to find information about parenting. Services, courses, leisure activities, family-friendly restaurants, and a website that is constantly updated. Subscribe to the newsletter if you will be in Milan for a longer period of time.

5 unforgettable experiences for
FOOTBALL LOVERS

411 **STADIO SAN SIRO**
Piazzale Angelo
Moratti
West ⑧
+39 02 4042 432
sansirostabium.com

Inside the stadium, the museum tells the story of the Milan and Inter teams through champions' jerseys and shoes, trophies and memorabilia. Combine the tour with a visit of the stadium, when there are no events and games in progress. Do check in advance.

411 STADIO SAN SIRO

412 CASA MILAN

Via Aldo Rossi 8
West ⑧
+39 02 6228 4545
casamilan.acmilan.com

Another museum dedicated solely to AC Milan fans, by Casa Milan, where children can participate in fun-educational itineraries thanks to 14 touch screens, find all the merch at the store and eat with their parents in the Casa Milan Bistrot. A full 'red-and-black' immersion.

413 MILAN STORE

AT: GALLERIA SAN CARLO
Corso Vittorio
Emanuele II
Duomo-San Babila ②
+39 02 2630 3235
store.acmilan.com

From onesies to teddy bears wearing the Milan jersey, to a plush ball, tracksuits and bathrobes for older kids and adults. Many of the official products can be customised on the spot for a fun gift. In the city centre or available online.

414 INTER STORE

Galleria Passarella 2
Duomo-San Babila ②
+39 02 2630 3235
store.inter.it

The team colours black and blue make up the theme of this store, which offers a whole range of gadgets for the fans of Inter, founded in 1908. From smartphone covers and caps to backpacks and sportswear, as well as mugs and signed shirts.

415 ARENA CIVICA / ARENA GIANNI BRERA

AT: PARCO SEMPIONE
Viale Giorgio Byron 2
Cairoli-Castello ③
fondoambiente.it

The arena is named after Gianni Brera, a journalist and sports writer. But the arena is Italy's oldest stadium and home to Inter Milan for over twenty years. Here the first championship, the first pennant, and the first Italian Cup were won. Long before Inter, the arena was once filled with water, hosting naval battles.

LAFAVIA MILANO

25 PLACES TO SLEEP

The 5 best
BUDGET HOTELS

416 OSTELZZZ

Via Giorgio Jan 5
Porta Venezia ⑤
+39 333 163 0121
ostelzzz.com

Ostelzzz was established by ZZZleep-andGo, a start-up founded by three 26-year-olds, which offers sleeping cabins in the Malpensa and Milan Orio al Serio airports. At Ostelzzz you sleep in 'capsules', but you're in the city centre. They also have a common area for socialising. There are 100 cabins as well as a few standard rooms.

417 OSTELLO BELLO

Via Medici 4
5vie ②
+39 02 3658 2720
ostellobello.com

There's a second branch, at the Central Station. But this hostel is a stone's throw from the Duomo and Colonne di San Lorenzo, one of the liveliest places around aperitivo time. Hang around at the hostel, where you can have a drink and tuck in to a rich buffet. Named Best Hostel of Italy.

418 BABILA HOSTEL

Via Conservatorio 2-A
Porta Romana ②
+39 344 003 7423
babilahostel.it

This hostel has a furnished terrace with a view over the rooftops of Milan. This hostel was inaugurated in 2017, after a thorough renovation of an institute founded in 1896 by the then Cardinal of Milan. This modern facility also has private rooms. Concerts and events in the bistro.

419 MADAMA HOSTEL & BISTROT

Via Benaco 1
South-East ⑦
+39 02 3672 7370
madamahostel.com

A former police station, transformed in 2015 into a hostel near the Prada Foundation. In an area that still lacks bars and restaurants, it serves good food, at shared tables, and welcomes non-guests. Frequented by musicians: the club downstairs, managed by the same team, hosts live music events.

420 GOGOL' OSTELLO & CAFTÈ LETTERARIO

Via Chieti 1
North-West ⑩
+39 02 3675 5522
gogolostellomilano.com

Not just a modern and colourful hostel, with designer objects and modern antiques, but also a venue for meetings, exchanges and friendships in the literary cafe, where book presentations, exhibitions, theatre performances and literary aperitifs are organised. It has four bedrooms with bathrooms and two dormitories.

417 OSTELLO BELLO

5 stylish
BOUTIQUE HOTELS

---

421 STRAFHOTEL&BAR

Via San Raffaele 3
Duomo-San Babila ②
+39 02 805 081
straf.it

Its interior design is quite unusual for a hotel. The architect De Cotiis used recycled and industrial materials, adding arte povera pieces and turning the 64 high-tech rooms into minimalist spaces. Much loved by the fashion world, also for the street bar, where there's often an aperitivo with a DJ set.

425 SAVONA 18 SUITES

422 NYX HOTEL MILAN

Piazza IV Novembre 3
North-East ⑤
+39 02 2217 5500
nyx-hotels.it/milan

Near Milan's Central Station, this building from 1949, which was home to Philips, has become a 4-star hotel with 299 rooms. The idea is to create an environment in which local artists are protagonists, such as in the gallery that sells works by Milanese street artists. Even the furnishings are made in Italy.

423 ROOM MATE GIULIA HOTEL

Via Silvio Pellico 4
Duomo-San Babila ②
+39 02 8088 8900
room-matehotels.com/
it/giulia

This place, which is located in a historic building from the 19th century, immediately makes you feel at home. The common areas and the 85 rooms were designed by the artist Patricia Urquiola, complete with designer furniture and inspired by Milan. Near the Duomo and La Scala.

424 HOTEL VIU MILAN

Via Aristotile
Fioravanti 6
North-West ⑩
+39 02 8001 0910
hotelviumilan.com

This design hotel boasts the most sought-after rooftop terrace with a bar and swimming pool of the moment, but it's exclusively reserved for clients and some private events. The eight floors, with 124 rooms, spa and hall, are all designed by Molteni. Chef Giancarlo Morelli runs the restaurant.

425 SAVONA 18 SUITES

Via Savona 18
Porta Genova ⑨
+39 02 2555 201
savona18suites.it

Housed in a typical Milanese tenement, this building was carefully renovated by Aldo Cibic, who wanted to give the structure a more contemporary feel without ruining it. Design and art fill all the spaces, with vintage objects in the 43 rooms.

5
CHARMING PLACES
to spend the night

---

426 MAISON MILANO I UNA ESPERIENZE

Via Giuseppe
Mazzini 4
Duomo-San Babila ②
+39 02 726 891
gruppouna.it

Very centrally located, though not too flashy. At the corner of Piazza Duomo, the UNA Maison Milano has only 27 rooms, a light and airy feel, and a room that can be reached via a second elevator, leading to a romantic penthouse suite. For a date night, overlooking the Madonnina.

427 PALAZZO SEGRETI

Via San Tomaso 8
Cairoli-Castello ③
+39 02 4952 9250
palazzosegreti.com

All 18 rooms of the very centrally located Palazzo Segreti have a longstanding history, which is accentuated with a few design items, four-posters, and some colour. The suites, located in another area, that is just a stone's throw from the Porta Nuova skyscrapers at Via Maurizio Quadrio 15, are also impeccably furnished.

428 SANTA MARTA SUITES

Via Santa Marta 4
5vie ②
+39 02 4537 3369
santamartasuites.com

Hidden in the alleys of old Milan, a living room with fireplace, original floors and antique wooden larch drawers extend a warm welcome to the guests of this recently restored house. The flat with dining corner, suites and rooms with contemporary accents on the walls are nice. They also have a rooftop terrace.

429 MAISON BORELLA

Alzaia Naviglio
Grande 8
Porta Genova ⑨
+39 02 5810 9114
hotelmaisonborella.com

This four-star hotel, in a former tenement with an inner courtyard, overlooks the Navigli. Thanks to the soundproofing, it's very quiet, and has retained its quaint, old allure. Ceilings with exposed beams, wood panelling and stylish furniture. Bright and with hardwood floors.

430 ANTICA LOCANDA DEI MERCANTI

Via San Tomaso 6
Cairoli-Castello ③
+39 02 8054 080
locanda.it

The severity of the 18th-century building is attenuated by the light interior. The 15 rooms are furnished with immaculate fabrics and have light wooden furniture and floors. Three rooms have a terrace, with plenty of flowers, where guests can enjoy breakfast or a drink before dinner. All are bright and quiet, some have a kitchenette.

427 PALAZZO SEGRETI

5 nice B&Bs WITH OPEN-AIR SPACE

431 ROSSOSEGNALE B&B

Via Sacchini 18
East ⑥
+39 02 2952 7453
rossosegnale.it

In the garden district, in an early-20th-century building, this unique hospitality project has three rooms, a small gallery, 3001 LAB, with a mezzanine floor for exhibitions by young emerging artists and a terrace with a solarium. The RossoSegnale Milano LOFT in Ticinese, a former photo studio, is also theirs.

432 LAFAVIA MILANO

Via Carlo Farini 4
North-West ⑩
+39 347 784 2212
lafaviamilano.com

Located in a 19th-century building, not far from the Isola area and the Porta Nuova district. It has just 4 rooms, which are all furnished with refined modern antiques and design. A delicious breakfast with organic products is served in the veranda with hanging garden on summer mornings.

433 BRONZINO HOUSE

Via Bronzino 20
East ⑥
+39 334 388 6892
bronzinohouse.it

In the attic of a typical Milanese house from the early 1900s, there are two double bedroom apartments, which overlook an inner courtyard, each of which has its own private bathroom. A bright living room with a small kitchenette for breakfast overlooks the terrace. Vintage furnishings and Frette linens.

434 LA TERRAZZA DI ROMEO

Via Giulio Uberti 5
East ⑥
+39 366 275 1233

A building in the Città Studi district – a lively area around the university – conceals a well-kept house with antique furniture and a terrace. Breakfast is particularly nice here: you can have it outside, and it's served on pretty china with pewter carafes.

435 TROVAILTEMPO

Via Novara 216
West ⑧
+39 339 502 1730
trovailtempo.it

The manager, Barbara, is passionate about art and journalism. She converted a tenement with a garden into a romantic retreat with 4 rooms, connected two by two, which each have a kettle and a fridge stuffed with fresh products for breakfast, like at home. There is also a large apartment with a full kitchen. The Atelier dei Sogni sells French-style objects and custom-made tablecloths.

5 *places to stay and*
FEEL AT HOME

436 CAMPERIO SUITES & APARTMENTS
Via M. Camperio 9
Cairoli-Castello ③
+39 02 3032 2800
camperio.com

A women's project, which owes its existence to the aesthetic sensibility of Lesley Severgnini and her designer mother Kazuko Hase. The beauty of the rooms, which are furnished with unique pieces, antiques and design objects, is well suited to this antique building, which has several homes with a kitchen and living room.

437 BRERA APARTMENTS
VARIOUS LOCATIONS
+39 02 3655 6284
brerapartments.com

Apartments are increasingly in demand, as they ensure independence, privacy and an insider's feel. Brera Apartments has houses in different areas of the city, all centrally located: Duomo, San Babila, Brera, up to Corso Garibaldi, Porta Venezia and Porta Romana.

438 ADORABILE
Via Bramante 14
Chinatown ⑩
+39 392 739 8826
adorabile.it

In this 1930s building, Adorabile's room names all have a link with the city. Zafran (once the kitchen) alludes to the main ingredient in *risotto alla milanese*, while Palchitt takes its cue from the stages of La Scala, combining vintage, contemporary style and design.

439 **LA CASA DI ALICE**

Via Galvano
Fiamma 40
East ⑥
+39 02 7012 3253
residence
lacasadialice.it

In an elegant area, close to the centre but also conveniently located for passengers arriving from the Linate airport, and where a direct metro stop will soon be added, this residence has 15 two-room apartments and a studio apartment for short-term rentals. All decorated with design objects. The lobby is perfect for reading and sipping a relaxing coffee.

440 **CIPROSETTE**

Via Cipro 7-1
East ⑥
ciprosette.it

In a well-served residential area, just a 10-minute journey by tram from the Duomo, Ciprosette has three housing solutions. A double bedroom with a bathroom, a studio with a giant photo of the Galleria, and a two-room apartment; the latter also has a fully equipped kitchen. Thanks to the owners' advice and the lively area you'll live like real locals.

436 **CAMPERIO SUITES & APARTMENTS**

TREKKING AMONG ARCHITECTURE

35 WEEKEND ACTIVITIES

---

5 shops where you can
LEARN

441 LES CHOURETTES

Corso San Gottardo 8,
inner courtyard,
buzzer 22
South-West ⑨
+39 348 918 4130
leschourettes.it

Ester and Stella called their shop
'Les Chourettes', a reference to the
word *'sciurette'*, a diminutive in Milanese
dialect for 'ladies', whose dresses are tailor-
made. And this place is one step up from
a tailor's shop. Because here, you can learn
to make clothes and accessories. Ready to
operate your own sewing machine?

442 LE MERCERIE DAL 1987

Via Terraggio 21
Sant'Ambrogio ④
+39 02 4770 2726

Passementerie, quills, threads and buttons
of all colours. If you love embroidery and
sewing, then you will also find something
you like here. The owner Sabine also
organises classes, teaching women how
to finish clothes with a scallop stitch,
cross-stitching, and lace, including items
for children, which you can choose in
the baby corner.

443 SPAZIO BATTIBALENO

Via Padova 244
North-East ⑤
+39 02 2305 5660
spaziobattibaleno.it

In un battibaleno means 'in the wink of an eye'. Here you can find tools and hobby materials, but the space also offers courses and workshops. You can learn – in person or online – how to make paper art or objects in wool and felt, and how to work with ceramic powder or resins, among other things. The only limit is your imagination.

444 SPAZIO B**K

Via L.P.
Lambertenghi 20
Isola ⑩
+39 02 8706 3126
spaziobk.com

Chiara, a librarian, and Diletta, a bookseller, have opened a workshop-bookshop with new and used illustrated books for children and adults as well as graphic and design books. They also host workshops and courses about the language of imagery. Also a good place to shop for self-published books and artisanal stationery.

445 BRICHECO

AT: LA STECCA
Via G. De Castillia 26
Isola ⑩
bricheco.org

Ever dreamt of having your own woodshop with all the tools? Then this is the perfect place for you: an association where work involves teaching each other skills and assisting one another. And where courses are held to learn or increase your dexterity. Also for children.

5 places for
SPORTS

---

446 SKIING
IN: BORMIO, LIVIGNO
AND STELVIO PASS
bormioski.eu
skipasslivigno.com
valtellina.it

The nearby ski resorts of Bormio, which
are home of the Ski World Cup, and
Santa Caterina Valfurva are very popular.
Livigno, the highest European plateau,
which is like an Italian 'Lapland', is
further abreast, but you can also go
on snowmobe and dog-sledding tours.
Go to the Stelvio Pass in summer.

447 TREKKING ITALIA
Via Santa Croce 2
Ticinese ②
+39 02 8372 838
trekkingitalia.org/
web/lombardia

Go walking for one (or more) days with
company. Trekking Italia, an association
created to 'approach, discover, respect
and defend nature' has a very active
Milan section, which also organises city
treks and group outings in the nearby
mountains and at the seaside.

448 YOGA FESTIVAL
yogafestival.it

Yoga mania hit Milan some time ago, in
part thanks to the autumn festival, which
includes conferences, seminars, classes
and meetings. They are divided into
different sections: tradition, innovation,
contemporary practices, and discovery.
Internationally known teachers are invited.

449 JOY MOVES

Via Valparaiso 9
South-West ⑨
+39 351 9888 383
joymoves.it

One of the newest activities, taught by Roberta Pedretti – one of the first people to bring it to Italy – is Eldoa, a technique studied by a French osteopathic doctor, which is beneficial for those with back problems and for prevention. They also offer a yoga wall, gyrotonic and TRX.

450 LOTUS POCUS

Via Guglielmo
Pepe 26
Isola ⑩
+39 393 9844 025
lotuspocus.com

Located in the vibrant Isola district, close to the metro, this studio is run by Tess Privett, a Hatha yoga instructor who teaches courses in Italian and English. They also practice other disciplines. The emphasis is on personal growth.

446 LIVIGNO

5 ways to
GET AROUND

---

451 TREKKING AMONG ARCHITECTURE

Piazza Gae Aulenti
North-West ⑩

Stairs, walkways, ascents, descents: in trainers, on skates or a bike (there are lifts anyway). Practicing sports among new architecture is fun. Start from the Diamant Tower, by Kohn Pedersen Fox, then head for the Unicredit Tower by César Pelli and then down towards the Isola district. Look up at the Vertical Forest by Stefano Boeri Architetti, after which you'll find yourself at I.M. Pei's Palazzo Lombardia.

452 NAVIGLIO MARTESANA

North-East ⑤

As the weather warms up, it's filled with athletes, cyclists, and families who feel like a walk. The starting point is at Cassina de' Pomm (Viale Gioia 194), where a wisteria covers the façade of a *bar-trattoria*. From here, follow the Naviglio on the bike trail, to reach Lecco on Lake Como for example. You can also stop at Tranvai (Via Tirano/Via Zuretti 71), at an old tram that has been turned into a kiosk.

453 DOCKYARD ITINERARY

BY: NAVIGAMI

Alzaia Naviglio
Grande 4
Porta Genova ⑨
+39 02 867 131
navigami.com

You embark on the Alzaia Naviglio Grande, near the Vicoli dei Lavandai (Laundrymen's Alley), and continue past Palazzo Galloni and the church of San Cristoforo. The way back takes you under the bridge of the 'Scodellino', up to the dock, and from here on to Naviglio Pavese, and finally through the Conchetta lock with its doors designed by Leonardo da Vinci. Duration: one hour.

454 TRENO BLU

+39 338 857 7210
ferrovieturistiche.it/
it/trenoblu

A puffing locomotive and its vintage 1930s carriages takes tourists on a journey through time, at a leisurely pace, winding its way along the course of the river Oglio, to Lake Iseo. You can stop in one of the restaurants to taste the typical roasted tench (a fish) or sail to Montisola.

455 CASCINA GUZZAFAME

Cascina Guzzafame
Gaggiano
+39 345 059 2882
(petting zoo)
cascinaguzzafame.it

Take the car along the Naviglio to Gaggiano. You'll feel as if you left the city. Stop at the educational farm with its rustic *trattoria* and petting zoo, take a stroll in the vegetable garden or do a yoga class. Pop into the dairy shop before making your way back home.

5 tips for
LAKE COMO

---

456 COMO-CABLE CAR TO BRUNATE
visitcomo.eu

The Duomo, with its late Gothic façade and dome by Juvarra, and the *Broletto* from the 1200s, with polychrome marble that was extracted from local quarries are situated inside the city walls. Our advice, however, is not to miss the 1930s rationalist architecture by Giuseppe Terragni. Be sure to take in the lake from above, on the cable car to Brunate.

457 STEAMER
STARTS AT: COMO
Navigazione Laghi
+39 800 551 801
navigazionelaghi.it

The most beautiful tour is that of the centre of the lake, aboard the recently restored historic steamer Concordia, sailing slowly past the villas of Bellagio, Varenna and Menaggio. Enquire at Aeroclub to experience the thrill of flying, with a water landing *(aeroclubcomo.com)*.

458 HIKING ABOVE TORNO
Torno (Como)

Torno is a small port, which can be reached by boat from Como. Leave the lake, the church and the bar behind you and climb up an old mule track. Magnificent views of the lake and mountains will open up to you as you climb higher, in the forests among ancient rural settlements in absolute silence.

459 THE SILK TRADITION
AT: MUSEO DIDATTICO DELLA SETA
Via Castelnuovo 9
Como
+39 031 303 180
museosetacomo.com

Spinning silk is a tradition that dates back to the 15th century. During the industrial revolution, this industry flourished on the shores of the lake, as you can see in the Silk Museum and in the interesting Museum of Textile Studies at the Ratti Foundation *(fondazioneratti.org)*. Advance booking required.

460 GARDENS OF THE VILLA DEL BALBIANELLO
Via Comoedia 5
Tremezzina (Como)
+39 034 456 110

Take the ferry from Varenna to the opposite bank and, descending towards Como, stop at Villa Balbianello. Its gardens and the villa are lovely and were used as a set for a *Star Wars* movie. You can also visit the town of Laglio and, who knows, maybe even spot George Clooney.

5
FOOD & WINE
experiences

―――――

461 FRANCIACORTA

franciacorta.net
franciacortainfiore.it

A weekend in the world's most famous vineyards, discovering the Franciacorta DOCG wines. Visit the cellars, some of which contain contemporary artworks, and the vineyards, stopping at castles and abbeys en route. The tour can also be done by bike, in the rolling hills that separate Rovato from Cazzago San Martino (about 60 km).

462 OLTREPÒ PAVESE

vinoltrepo.org

On the map, the outline of this area resembles a bunch of grapes. And you will see row after row of vines extending towards the Apennines among the farmsteads, 19th-century villas, parish churches and castles. Taste DOCG Oltrepò Pavese (traditional method) and Cruasé wines, as well as Bonarda from Oltrepò Pavese DOC, which pairs nicely with the typical salami of Varzi.

463 VALTELLINA

valtellina.it
valtellinawinetrail.com

Try cheese (Valtellina Casera and Bitto DOP), cured meats (bresaola IGP) and buckwheat pasta *(pizzoccheri)* with savoy cabbage, potatoes and local butter. Pair this with some great wines, produced with grapes that grow in inaccessible places. This is also where the 'Valtellina Wine Trail' autumn competition is held. Fratelli Ciapponi *(ciapponi.com)* in Morbegno sells all of the above and more.

464 MANTUA

turismo.mantova.it

Mantua is aristocratic and steeped in history, a city-court, built around the Ducal Palace, with its *Camera degli Sposi* frescoes by Mantegna. A culinary tradition that was handed down from this court is pumpkin tortelli with mustard and *amaretti. Sbrisolona,* a delicious crunchy almond cake, is absolutely delicious.

465 PARMA

HOP ON:
PARMA CITY HALL
Piazza Garibaldi 1
Parma
+39 052 121 8889
turismo.comune.
parma.it

How can you resist *Parmigiano Reggiano* and *Prosciutto di Parma?* Hop on the Tastybus, which leaves every day in front of the city hall, to visit the local dairies and ham factories. UNESCO declared Parma the City of Gastronomy, as it is the epicentre of the Italian Food Valley, and one of the destinations with the highest number of local products. A day trip that will whet your appetite...

5 ×

RELAXING

among villas and gardens

---

466 FONDAZIONE AUGUSTO RANCILIO
AT: VILLA ARCONATI
Via Fametta 1
Bollate (MI)
+39 393 868 0934
villaarconati-far.it

An 'Italian Versailles', which was completed at the end of the 18th century. The visit includes the museum and library, the monumental staircase that leads to the main floor, with scenes painted by the Galliari brothers, who were the set designers of the Teatro Ducale in Milan. The Red Room, in a neo-Gothic style, was restored a few years ago.

467 ROYAL VILLA OF MONZA
Viale Mirabellino 2
Monza (MB)
+39 039 224 0024
villarealedimonza.it

A palace surrounded by a centuries-old park, which was commissioned by Ferdinand of Habsburg as a country residence in 1777 from Giuseppe Piermarini. The rose garden is extraordinary, with 4000 varieties of roses. A must-see in May.

468 VILLA E COLLEZIONE PANZA
Piazza Litta 1
Varese (VA)
+39 033 228 3960
*fondoambiente.it/luoghi/
villa-e-collezione-panza*

Visit a delightful villa on the hill above Burmio, which is surrounded by an Italian garden, whose origins date back to the 1700s. Renowned for Count Giuseppe Panza's contemporary American art collection. The site-specific works can be found in the rustic wing.

469 FONDAZIONE IL VITTORIALE DEGLI ITALIANI

Via del Vittoriale 12
Gardone Riviera (BS)
+39 0365 296 511
vittoriale.it

In its garden, which is part of the Grandi Giardini Italiani network, you will come upon the keel of a ship, that extends into the lake. It's just one of the many peculiarities of this estate, which was developed by the poet Gabriele d'Annunzio in 1921–38. Visit the house, the Prioria and the museum in the park.

470 ISOLA BELLA – LAGO MAGGIORE

+39 032 393 3478
isoleborromee.it

An intimate experience awaits you, away from the noise and off the beaten track. Head to Isola Bella outside the tourist opening hours, for dinner at Fornello, a shop with a kitchen. Then spend the night in one of the apartments in the village – Borromeo's dream homes – in former fishermen's houses.

→ 467 ROYAL VILLA OF MONZA

5
UNESCO SITES
(out of 10 in Lombardy)

---

471 **BERGAMO**
CARRARA ACADEMY
Piazza Giacomo
Carrara 82
Bergamo (BG)
+39 035 234 396
lacarrara.it

The walls – which were built by the Republic of Venice from 1561 onwards, and which are just over 5 km long – became a UNESCO site in 2017. Follow them to the upper town, which you can also reach by funicular, to Piazza Vecchia, with the Colleoni Chapel, that Le Corbusier said was the most beautiful square in Italy. The marvellous Carrara Academy is located in lower Bergamo.

471 BERGAMO

472 VILLAGGIO CRESPI D'ADDA

Crespi d'Adda (BG)
+39 02 9098 7191
villaggiocrespi.it

This 'ideal company town' was built by the Crespi family, next to its textile factory, along the river Adda. The employees and their families had a house with a vegetable garden and a yard, as well as a communal indoor pool. Also worth visiting is the moving cemetery.

473 SANTA GIULIA MUSEUM

Via dei Musei 81-B
Brescia (BS)
+39 030 297 7833
bresciamusei.com/ santagiulia

Built in 753 AD by the Longobard King Desiderius, the Santa Giulia Museum is a former convent. Visit the Longobard basilica, the Romanesque oratory, the Choir of the nuns, the 16th-century church of Santa Giulia and the cloisters. The Pinacoteca Tosio Martinengo, with works by Raphael, Romanino, Hayez and Canova, is also worth a visit.

474 SABBIONETA

turismo.mantova.it

Along with Mantua, which is also on the UNESCO heritage list, Sabbioneta is one of the symbols of the Renaissance. This small 'independent state', an 'ideal city', was built from scratch in the second half of the 1500s by Vespasiano Gonzaga. The hexagonal city wall has been preserved.

475 CREMONA

turismocremona.it

The sound of violins resounds throughout the city, from over 150 violin shops and the Violin Museum. On special occasions, you can hear some of the historical instruments in the Auditorium, which has perfect acoustics. The Duomo and the Torrazzo, Europe's tallest brick tower, are also worth visiting.

"LUNGO COME LA FABBRICA DEL DUOMO"

25 RANDOM FACTS AND URBAN DETAILS

5 ways to be
CONNECTED

---

476 PUBLIC TRANSPORT

atm-mi.it
atmosfera.atm.it

ATM has bus, tram and subway lines (four lines and a fifth currently being built). They sell single-journey tickets (90 minutes, with only one subway journey) or day passes. Getting to stops like Fiera in Rho will cost you more. You can calculate routes and distances on the website or using the app. At ATMosfera, you can have dinner at night while riding through the city. If you text ATM to 48444, your ticket will be sent to your mobile phone, so you don't have to queue.

477 BIKES

bikemi.com
mobike.com

BikeMi, Mobike and ofo are Milan's bike-sharing services. The first one has fixed stops, mainly in the city centre, and requires a subscription (one day, month, year, you're charged after the first half hour); the others are free floating meaning you can take and leave bikes anywhere with the app and you pay depending on your use.

478 CAR SHARING

car2go.com
enjoy.eni.com
e-vai.com
site.sharengo.it
(electric)
it.drive-now.com
ubeeqo.com/it

Various car-sharing options and methods, many of which are free floating. All cars can access the C area (the restricted traffic area) and use the yellow (for residents) and blue (paid, but in this case without paying) parking spaces. You must have had your driving license for at least one year to rent a car.

479 RAILWAY

trenitalia.com
italotreno.it
trenord.it

Milan has two main railway stations. From Milano Centrale you can take fast, regional and local trains. The Trenord trains depart from Cadorna, with local and regional trains to, for example, Como. The stations are connected by the 'Passante underground railway', a metropolitan train system in the city for which you can use your ATM ticket.

480 AIRPORTS

milanomalpensa-airport.com
milanolinate-airport.com
milanbergamoairport.it

Malpensa, Linate and Orio al Serio are Milan's airports (the latter is near the city of Bergamo). The first can be reached with the Malpensa Express from Cadorna and by train or bus from Milan's Central Station. Here you'll also find buses to Orio al Serio. You can get to Linate by public transport, with bus 73 using a regular city ticket.

5
KEYS
to see the city

---

481 #DOMENICALMUSEO

beniculturali.it/
domenicalmuseo
abbonamentomusei.it

In Italy, every first Sunday of each month, all state-owned monuments, museums, galleries, archaeological sites, parks and monumental gardens can be visited for free (does not include private monuments/museums or foundations). For art lovers there's also a subscription to the museums of Lombardy, which grants access to more than 120 museums throughout the year.

482 TOURING CLUB ITALIANO

PUNTO TOURING
Corso Italia 26
Porta Romana ②
+39 02 8526 760
touringclub.it

The association, which has been working in tourism for over 120 years – publishing everything from maps and guidebooks to magazines, has over 280.000 members throughout the Italian peninsula. Thanks to the contribution of many volunteers, many urban spaces are open regularly: in Milan they take care of 16 spaces.

483 CORTILI APERTI A MILANO

ADSI-Associazione Dimore Storiche *dimorestoriche italiane.it*

A unique event to explore the splendid courtyards of some important Milanese historical residences, which are otherwise difficult to visit. Cortili Aperti is organised at the end of May, in conjunction with the opening of 300 historic houses, castles, villas, farmhouses, courtyards and gardens, throughout Italy, unveiling places of rare beauty to the public.

484 GIORNATE FAI

+39 02 4676 151 *fondoambiente.it*

For 25 years, every third weekend of March and October, FAI, the most important foundation for the protection and promotion of the Italian artistic and natural heritage, has been organising 'Le Giornate del FAI', when more than a thousand places throughout Italy are open to the public. The idea is to introduce people to the beauty of art, culture and history. Open to all. FAI members have exclusive entrances and preferential lanes.

485 MILANOCARD

milanocard.it

The Milan city pass, available in 24-, 48- and 72-hour versions, includes public transportation, audioguides and free tickets or discounts in 30 museums. There are over 200 attractions, including restaurants and shops. Children under the age of ten don't pay.

5

COLOURFUL
IDEAS

---

486 VILLA INVERNIZZI
Via Cappuccini 3
Porta Venezia ①

Hidden among the Milanese 'art nouveau streets', in front of Casa Berri-Meregalli by architect Giulio Ulisse Arata, there is an unexpected oasis called Villa Invernizzi. Its park, visible from the street, is home to a small community of pink flamingos that live there undisturbed. They are pampered by a caretaker.

487 ARTLINE
AT: CITYLIFE
Various accesses
West ⑧
artlinemilano.com

W.A.L.L. (Walls Are Love's Limits) is a 1000-square-metre artwork, a wall against walls, which the internationally-renowned Italian graffiti artist Eron created in 2018. It is part of ArtLine, urban art interspersed among the CityLife skyscrapers, and includes site-specific works by Riccardo Benassi, Judith Hopf, Matteo Rubbi and Serena Vestrucci.

488 ORTICA

East ⑥
orticamemoria.com

This used to be Milan's 'mob' district, featured in Italian singer Enzo Jannacci's songs and in De Sica's movie *Miracle in Milan*. It is set to become the first museum district. The buildings' façades will be covered by 20 murals: a story about the history and protagonists of the 20th century. Work has already been started by OR.ME Ortica Memoria and the first 11 walls have been painted.

489 MILANOARTE

milanoarte.net

The 'Colours of Milan: Street Art Itineraries with the Author' are the brainchild of Elena Stafano, who loves art, and MilanoArte. You'll be accompanied by well-known artists. The stops include Via Morosini, with a piece by Millo and Piazza della Repubblica with work by the American artist Zio Ziegler.

490 OFFICINA DEL COLORE

Via Giuseppe
Giacosa 39
NoLo ⑤
+39 02 2804 0489
officinadelcolore
milano.com

If you want to see life in colour, or maybe make it more colourful, head to Maurizio Marelli's shop. Here you will find a range of pigments, for painters, ceramists, and maybe even chefs, which are developed in a workshop outside the city. The owner will explain their uses and features.

5 *upcoming*
URBAN PROJECTS

491 REOPENING OF THE NAVIGLI

Canals, bridges, boats in the city centre? The city is thinking about reopening the historical Milanese canals, the Navigli, which were filled in between 1929 and the 1960s. The project spans from Cassina de' Pomm to the Darsena, following the course of the water. A dream, for many, that might become reality.

491 NAVIGLI

492 WILL THERE BE 5 CITYLIFE TOWERS?

Three of the planned skyscrapers have already been completed in the redeveloped site of the former trade fair. Daniel Libeskind's building was completed in autumn 2020. Rumours about a new competition to build two further buildings are becoming increasingly loud.

493 A 'NEW' POLITECNICO

The project to reform and reshape the Polytechnic University of Milan was designed by Renzo Piano and will be developed by ODB Architects. To make the area greener, the 'Submarine' building will be demolished, replacing it with a green area, flanked by new study spaces.

494 RAILWAY STATIONS, GREEN IDEAS

The idea is to rehabilitate the abandoned railway stations of Farini, Greco-Breda, Lambrate, Porta Romana, Rogoredo, Porta Genova and San Cristoforo and improve city traffic with a focus on sustainability, and a WWF nature reserve.

495 A 'CAMPUS FOR THE ARTS'

In one of the railway stations, at Farini. Thanks to a project by the Politecnico for the Brera Academy, the students' educational activities, which are currently scattered in various locations, will be grouped here. In the coming years, the project will be developed to include a campus, which will give Brera a second permanent location.

5

EXPRESSIONS / SAYINGS

496 **"TÀCCHES AL TRAM"**

Literally: latch yourself to the tram. Once the tram doors were open and they slowed down you could hop on. This expression is used to indicate to someone that a problem does not concern us and to 'suggest' that our interlocutor fends for himself and, more metaphorically, leaves.

497 **"ANDÀ A OFF"**

This means to freeload. This expression has a historical origin. In the 14th century the boats that carried construction materials for the Duomo were exempt from taxes and bore the inscription 'A.U.Fa.' that is, *Ad Usum Fabricae*. To avoid paying, people used the sign without permission.

498 **"LUNGO COME LA FABBRICA DEL DUOMO"**

This is said of a job that is far from completed. Work on the Venerable Factory of the Duomo, from the construction of the religious building in 1386 to the present day, has never ended. Over the years, the works have continued, with restoration, improvements, and safety upgrades.

499 **"OFFELLÉE FÀ EL TO MESTÉE"**

"Pastry chef do your job". We say this to those who, often presumptuously, want to teach others to do a job that is not really their own and therefore give (unsolicited) advice to others.

500 **"CHI VOLTA EL CUU A MILAN LE VOLTA AL PAN"**

The city has always been a place with plenty of job opportunities. Ignoring them, or leaving the city, means you can no longer earn a living. It's one of the many expressions that refer to the productivity of the capital of Lombardy.

INDEX

COLOPHON

EDITING *and* COMPOSING — Silvia Frau

TRANSLATION — Luisa Grigoletto

GRAPHIC DESIGN — Joke Gossé and doublebill.design

PHOTOGRAPHY — Massimo Ripani — massimoripani.it
and Giovanni Simeone — simephoto.com

COVER IMAGE — Pirelli HangarBicocca (secret 358) by Massimo Ripani

The addresses in this book have been selected after thorough independent
research by the author, in collaboration with Luster Publishing. The selection
is solely based on personal evaluation of the business by the author. Nothing
in this book was published in exchange for payment or benefits of any kind.

D/2022/12.005/11

ISBN 978 94 6058 3124

NUR 512, 510

© 2018 Luster Publishing, Antwerp
Second edition, May 2022 – First reprint, May 2022
lusterpublishing.com — THE500HIDDENSECRETS.COM
info@lusterpublishing.com

Printed in Italy by Printer Trento.